Capo Inventions

SOLO GUITAR MUSIC

FOR THE

3-STRING PARTIAL CAPO

◈

Harvey Reid

WOODPECKER
MULTIMEDIA

York, Maine USA

ISBN: 978-1-63029-002-3

Library of Congress Control# 2013951625

WOODPECKER
MULTIMEDIA

PO Box 815 York Maine 03909 USA

www.woodpecker.com

CONTENTS

WARNING- All the pieces in this book are meant to be played with a partial capo, as shown on page 3.

ABOUT HARVEY REID

Harvey Reid has been a full-time acoustic guitar player since 1974, and has performed over 6000 concerts throughout the US and in Europe. He won the 1981 National Fingerpicking Guitar Competition (without using a partial capo) and the 1982 International Autoharp contest, and has released 28 highly-acclaimed recordings of original, traditional and contemporary acoustic music, as well as a concert DVD.

He is best known for his solo fingerstyle guitar work, but he is also a solid flatpicker (he won Bill Monroe's *Beanblossom* bluegrass guitar contest in 1976), a versatile singer, lyricist, prolific composer, arranger and songwriter. He also plays mandolin and bouzouki. Reid recorded the first album ever of 6 & 12-string banjo music, and his CD *Solo Guitar Sketchbook* made Guitar Player Magazine's Top 20 essential acoustic guitar CD's list. His CD *Steel Drivin' Man* was chosen by Acoustic Guitar Magazine as one of Top 10 Folk CD's of all time, along with *Woody Guthrie, Ry Cooder* and other hallowed names. His music was included in the blockbuster BBC TV show *Musical Tour of Scotland*, and Reid was featured in the Rhino Records *Acoustic Music of the 90's* collection, along with a "who's who" line-up of other artists including *Richard Thompson, Jerry Garcia & Leo Kottke.*

In 1980 Reid published *A New Frontier in Guitar,* the first book about the partial capo, and in 1984 he wrote *Modern Folk Guitar,* the first college textbook for folk guitar. Until now, his 1983 book *Sleight of Hand* has been the only published book of arrangements for partially-capoed guitar. He is the first to publish and record with the partial capo, and is responsible for most of what is known about the device. He lives in southern Maine with his family.

ABOUT THE MUSIC IN THIS BOOK

All the music in this book requires a 3-string partial capo similar to these.

Shubb "c7b"   *Kyser "Short Cut"*   *Liberty FLIP Model 43*

The capo is a common device that has been used for centuries to clamp across a guitar fretboard to raise the pitch of all six strings. It is used primarily to change the key when accompanying vocals and other instruments, but can also be used to change the timbre of the instrument.

I have been exploring the partial capo since 1976, though I greatly enjoy playing guitar without one and also regularly use a number of non-standard tunings. I have found no evidence that any type of partial capo has been used traditionally other than the 5th string capo on a banjo. I am not aware of any guitar recordings made with one earlier than my own first record *"Nothin' but Guitar"* in 1982, or of any published transcriptions that preceded my 1983 book *"Sleight of Hand."* Many thousands of guitar players are now using the device, and it now appears that it has passed out of the experimental phase and taken permanent hold as a new tool for musicians of all levels. It is not useful in all kinds of music: it behaves much like an open tuning, and the droning resonances it offers are well-suited for folk, celtic, bluegrass and some country songs. It has not proven particularly helpful in jazz, swing, ragtime, or music with a lot of root movement. It has been used effectively in arranging some classical pieces.

The arrangements and compositions included here are representative of a substantial body of music I have created for the partial capo. This music sounds "right" to my ears and feels guitaristic and natural to my hands. I have also used the partial capo to arrange a considerable number of traditional melodies. I prefer them to other ways I have been able to play them, and I think this speaks quite favorably for the partial capo's value. To date, my 19 recordings feature 101 songs and instrumentals that use 14 different configurations of a partial capo. Most of them are in standard tuning, though a few use both a partial capo and a non-standard tuning. I have done a few things with multiple partial capos, but decided to include in this book a body of instrumental music for solo guitar that only uses the most popular and approachable partial capo device, the *Esus* partial capo, which I have used on all but 12 of my partial capo recordings. The pieces here range in difficulty from quite easy to difficult, and are primarily folk, Celtic and classically flavored.

The TAB and fingerings in this book were carefully done by musician Jeff Hickey. We sat in the same room, and played through them slowly for many days, making every effort to make sure that the fingerings are notated exactly as I play them. All the pieces in this book except the *Norway Suite* are played in standard tuning. The music in this book generally progresses in difficulty with the easier tunes at the beginning.

Harvey Reid (York, Maine, 2006)

3

ABOUT THE PARTIAL CAPO

The partial capo is a quick and easy way to change the limits of what is possible on the guitar. It works in much the same way that non-standard or "open" tunings do, and offers a new landscape of voicings and fingerings, but with several important differences. Its effect is greatest in solo guitar situations, where the extra resonance of having an extra string or two ringing can be dramatic. In a group setting, the advantages are less obvious, though certainly it can provide a richer sound.

Since you generally use a partial capo without changing the tuning, the geometry of the fingerboard remains the same as standard tuning. Chord shapes and scale patterns remain familiar, but you can get the rich, droning sound of an open tuning without re-learning the fingerboard. Secondly, when you actually put the guitar in a different tuning, it is not really possible to sound like you are in standard tuning, and it can even be hard to make chords like minors and diminished. It's hard to get out of the "drone zone" in a full open tuning, but if you use a simulated "tuning" done with a partial capo, you can achieve the drone sound of the tuning, but also can easily switch back to a "normal" guitar sound, and everything in-between. Standard tuning evolved because it offers a remarkable number of ways to play chords and scales, and the closed position scales and the lifetime of left-hand fingerings you learn are lost when you change the tuning.

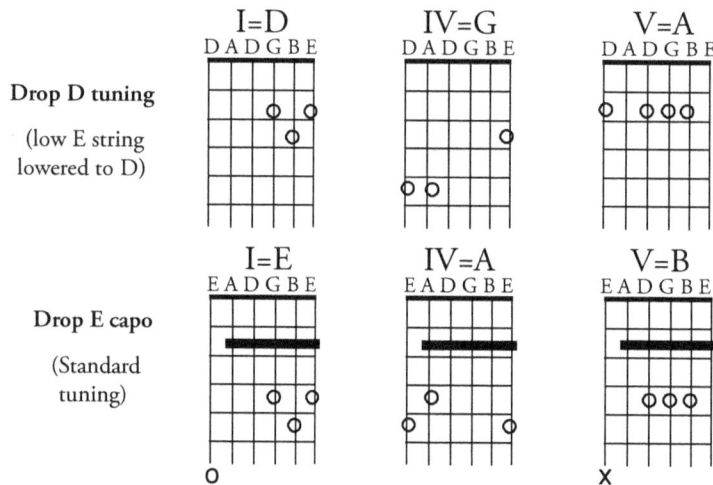

Showing the I, IV and V chords in the key of D in Drop D tuning as compared to the Drop E partial capo illustrates how the chord shapes do not change with the partial capo they way they do when you change the tuning.

ESUS OR E SUSPENDED CONFIGURATION

Though there are dozens of ways to play guitar with a partial capo, this book focuses on the most popular form, usually known as an *Esus* or "E-suspended" capo, because in standard tuning the capo forms an E suspended 4 or E-suspended chord: EBEABE. This configuration bears many similarities to the common DADGAD tuning, where strings 1, 2 and 6 are lowered a whole step below standard pitch. The three most common mechanisms are shown below. Usually the guitar is kept in standard tuning, though some people use the *Esus* capo in DADGAD tuning. All but 3 of the pieces in this book use the Esus configuration.

Esus configuration with an adjustable **Third Hand Capo®**, which can clamp any combination of strings on any guitar by rotating the cams, but is hard to reach over.

Esus configuration with the **G7 Newport #3** partial capo, which allows easy access behind and around it.

Esus configuration with the **SpiderCapo** partial capo. It is hard to reach over for notes on the low strings.

Except for perhaps the *Dropped-E* capo, where only the top 5 strings are clamped at fret 2, the Esus configuration is the partial capo form used the most often by guitarists of all levels. It is used to teach children, beginners, and those with disabilities to play guitar chords using only 1 finger of the left hand, yet is also the capo configuration most commonly used by songwriters and advanced instrumentalists. The first pieces of music I know of that used it were written by me in 1982 and released on my 2nd LP *A Very Old Song* in 1984. They include the Suite in F, *Dreamer or Believer* and the title cut *A Very Old Song*. These were done with the *Third Hand Capo*, though by 1984 I was playing most things with a sawed-off and modified *Shubb*® capo similar to the one shown above, which allows better access around and behind the capo. My first LP, *Nothin' but Guitar*, released in September 1982, was the first recording I know of that used the partial capo, though it did not feature the *Esus* configuration.

OPEN A AND ASUS CONFIGURATIONS

Any of the *Esus* capos shown previously can be flipped around to clamp only strings 2, 3 and 4, to form an ordinary A chord. This capo configuration I call **Open A** (because of its resemblance to *Open A* tuning), and if the B string is tuned one half-step sharp to C, with the capo still in *Open A* configuration, it forms a configuration I call **A suspended** or simply **Asus**. This is used on the *Norway Suite* (which is in this book), and several other of my works, including *Pegasus*, *The Great Sad River*, and *I Have Finally Found a Home* (which are not in this book.)

The *Shubb*® Esus capo flipped around to form *Open A* or *Asus*.

COMPARING ESUS CONFIGURATION & DADGAD TUNING

Though the *Esus* capo configuration, which forms the chord EBEABE, seems to resemble the common DADGAD tuning very closely, there are important differences. They are a whole step apart: DADGAD is most often used to play in D and its related keys, and in *Esus* you most often play in E. If you are a singer, this is vital, or if you are accompanying fiddlers or other instruments. You must tune your whole guitar down a whole step or use a baritone guitar in order to use the *Esus* capo and still sound in D, which can be a disadvantage.

Not only are the chord forms and scales in *Esus* the same as standard tuning (because you are in standard) but there are subtler differences. DADGAD offers fewer closed chord positions, and almost no "closed position" (movable) scale patterns. The change of tuning spreads the scales out over a much wider reach for the left hand, and there is no way to avoid this fact. In my opinion,

after examining both of them carefully, I think it is easier in Esus than in DADGAD to play fast scale work with the fingers, supported by bass notes or chords, (such as you would with in arranging a fingerpicked fiddle tune) and it is also possible to play solo guitar arrangements that feature the use of moving counterpoint bass lines. This is one of the defining features of solo classical guitar, for example, and several of the pieces in this book are a very deliberate attempt to show how to play melody and bass lines at the same time, while still maintaining the lovely and seductive richness of the open drone strings.

In *Esus*, you can generally arrange most melodies in two octaves, something you rarely hear in DADGAD.

ABOUT THE NOTATION IN THIS BOOK

This book is written in both TAB and standard notation, because neither alone tells you enough about the music. This practice has become commonplace for guitar music because the notation does not adequately describe the left-hand fingerings, and the TAB does not show the melodic and chordal structure or the timing and duration of the notes. I sometimes use classical guitar symbols: p i m a for right hand fingers, and Roman numerals above the staff to indicate barre chords. Above each music staff is a number that represents the measure number, so we can refer to a particular measure.

The partial capo presents some difficult choices of its own regarding notation.

The capo position is shown with black rectangles on the TAB staff, with a numeral (always a 2 in this book) to indicate the fret where the capo is placed. The standard notation here is written the way the music sounds. It may "feel" like you are playing in D position, with the capo 2, but you really are sounding in E, and the staff will have 4 sharps to indicate the key of E. Some classical guitar music (especially that which uses Drop D tuning, where only the bass string differs from standard tuning) is written to be played as if it were in standard tuning, as a convenience to guitar sight-readers, and to the confusion of others.

There is a serious unresolved issue about whether TAB is counted from the capo or from the nut. Because guitar players who use capos "think" from the capo rather than the nut, I have always done my TAB this way, and as the first person to publish partial capo sheet music I feel that it is counter-intuitive to do it otherwise. It becomes especially cumbersome to notate TAB as 9 and 10th fret numbers when you are just playing G and C chord shapes above a capo on the 7th fret.

This problem seems to stem from the fact that music notation computer programs do not seem to have been written to handle the partial capo, and the only way people can easily notate TAB that way is to count from the nut. My attempts to explain this problem to programmers who work for the guitar notation manufacturers have so far been fruitless, and my attempts to initiate a dialog to encourage publishers of guitar TAB to reach a collective decision on how this ought to be done have also failed. Musical arrangements are being published that count TAB numbers from the nut. This practice also makes an awkward situation of when the 0 or open string is used. To my mind, a fret 0 or open string is just that– unfretted by the left hand. TAB that is counted from the nut considers notes clamped by the capo to be other than 0 for their TAB numbers.

There is one problem that one sometimes encounters when counting TAB from the capo, and that is TAB that is under or below the capo. I use the ø Theta character in this book (a 0 with a slash through it, option-O on my keyboard) to indicate a fretted note at the same fret as the capo, and a negative fret number for the uncommon occasions when you actually reach over the capo to a lower fret. There are no negative TAB numbers in this book, though there is a ø in the first measure of the first song.

The TAB for this book was done by Jeff Hickey in the program *Finale*, and the incorrect, auto-generated guitar TAB numbers caused by the partial capo were replaced one at a time by hand.

There will be some slight discrepancies between the way the music is written on the page and the recorded versions I have done, but this reflects the changes in the way I now play things, or might have done on the day we transcribed the piece. There are always judgment calls to be made about which bass notes or grace notes to include, but it makes sense for me to make those calls rather than someone else. Also bear in mind that I like to tune my 6-string guitar down a half step to Eb (I like to sing in Eb and I like the extra resonance), so a number of these tunes will sound a half-step lower pitched on the recording.

THE SKYE BOAT SONG

ABOUT "THE SKYE BOAT SONG"

The Skye Boat Song is a simple, sparse arrangement that illustrates some of the defining features of the *Esus* configuration. The open string resonance is vital to creating the bagpipe-like drones that suit the song. To my ears, this song sounds best in a somewhat modal treatment, which means you don't really have full major or minor tonality, also consistent with the Scottish tradition of a melody played against a constant drone. I heard a sparse bagpipe version in Inverness, Scotland that guided me in this arrangement, and that sound rings more true to me than the strummed-chord folk song versions you most often hear played on the guitar. To my ears, the richest part is not the opening measure where the bass note is the tonic E, but the next one when the melody is played against the open A string or 5th. This is the classic bagpipe drone sound. This arrangement also allows other vital bass notes (the 4 and the 6) to sound against the ringing melody notes, and you have the feeling of chord changes and root movement that can get lost in a total drone arrangement. The bagpipe does not supply the 4 or 6 bass note (on fret 2 of the A string) which is very welcome here in implying the IV major and the ii minor chords. This arrangement is quite easy, though keeping the long notes ringing can take some control.

*(Recorded on WP#114 **Guitar Voyages** in 2000.)*

ABOUT "THE HIGHWIRE HORNPIPE"

The *Highwire Hornpipe* is what you might call an exercise or an étude (which is French for study), since it is a melody played with the fingers, fretted entirely on the high E string, and played against a droning, open-string bass. Technically, you could play this piece in any tuning, but the strings that are not being fretted resonate sympathetically as you play the guitar, and the faint Esus chord that rings underneath this piece helps make it work. The plaintive drone of a sus4 chord is something we associate with Celtic guitar music.

On the recorded version of this piece, I play it on a 12-string guitar that is tuned 3 steps low, so it actually sounds in C#. The piece works fine on a 6-string, though if I have the choice I choose the 12-string.

The 1st section of the piece is a fiddle-tune AABB form with a slower melody, and the 2nd half is also an AABB, but with a much faster melody line. The slower melody part is actually played with only one finger of each hand. Oddly enough, I use the ring finger of the right hand to play it, and the 2nd finger of the left hand, though I suppose there would be nothing wrong with using a different finger of either hand if it suited you. The left hand finger stays on the fingerboard, and the melody notes are all slurs and slides, almost like a dulcimer. In measure 1, I pluck the string once for the 2nd fret note, then slide down to the ø note, and then a pull-off sounds the open string. The next ascending phrase also sounds 3 notes with just one plucked note. A hammer-on and a slide then add the other 2.

The faster section requires some left hand agility, especially with the 4th finger. In measure 31 you have the 1st finger on the 5th fret (above the capo) and then you trill the 7th fret (I use the 2nd finger for this) and then the 10th fret (with the 4th finger.) I leave the 1st finger in place on the 5th fret, but if your reach can't span 5 frets you can jump up and then back down and you won't lose much. On the final phrase of the B part of the 2nd half (measure 52), you play frets 3, 5 and 7 as a triplet and then play fret 8. I use left-hand fingers 1, 2 and 4 for the triplet, and then slide the 4th finger up to the 8th fret and then back down to 7.

When I perform this I usually speed up the 2nd half for the last time through. The way this piece is constructed it can be played very fast and has a lot of drive, which is what fiddle tunes are all about. We guitarists have spent many years trying to play fiddle fingerings on a guitar fingerboard at high speeds, and it is refreshing to play a "fiddle tune" that was created for the guitar.

(Recorded on WP#105 Solo Guitar Sketchbook in 1989. Also on DVD-01 One April Night in 2004)

THE HIGHWIRE HORNPIPE

9

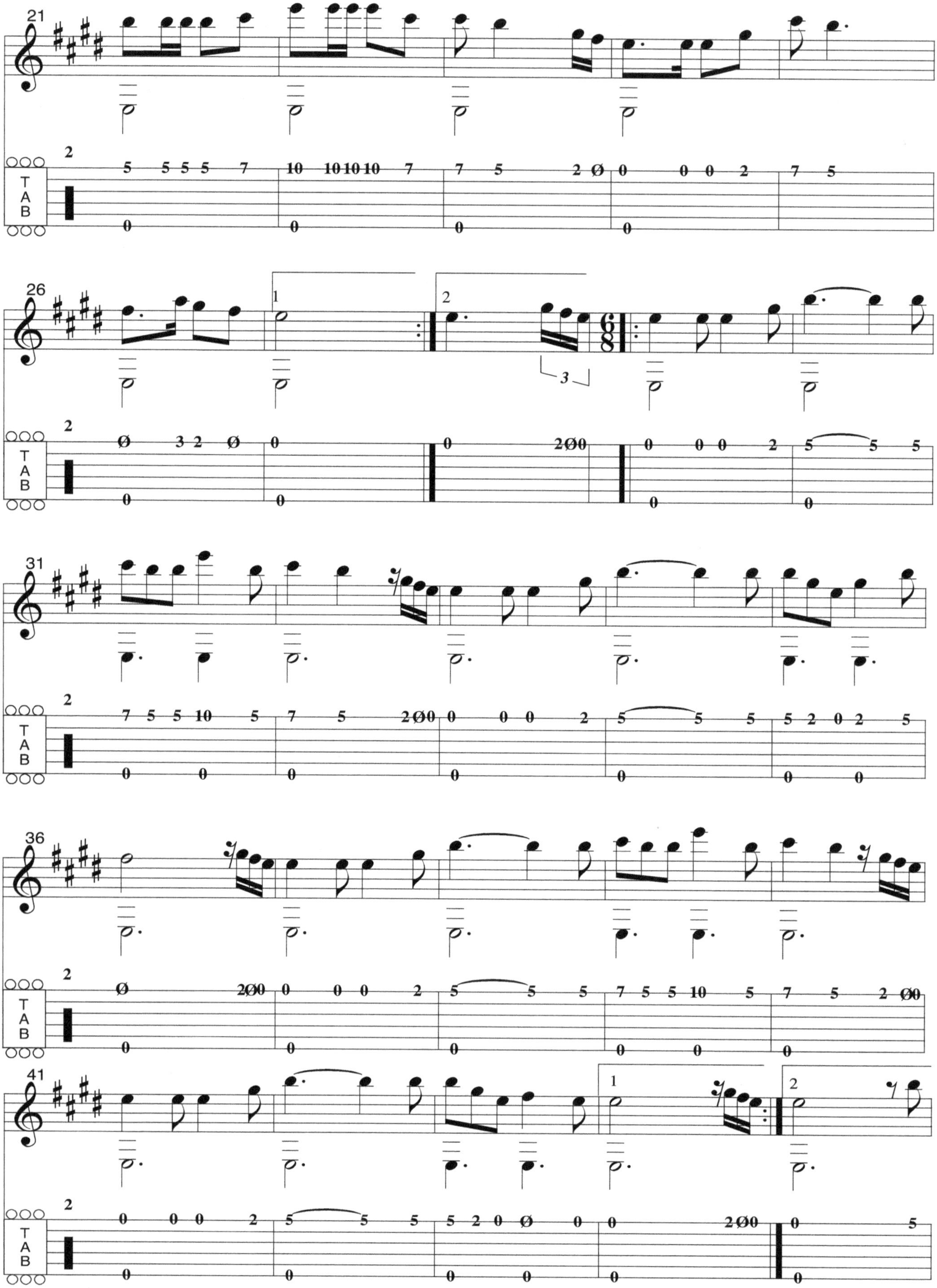

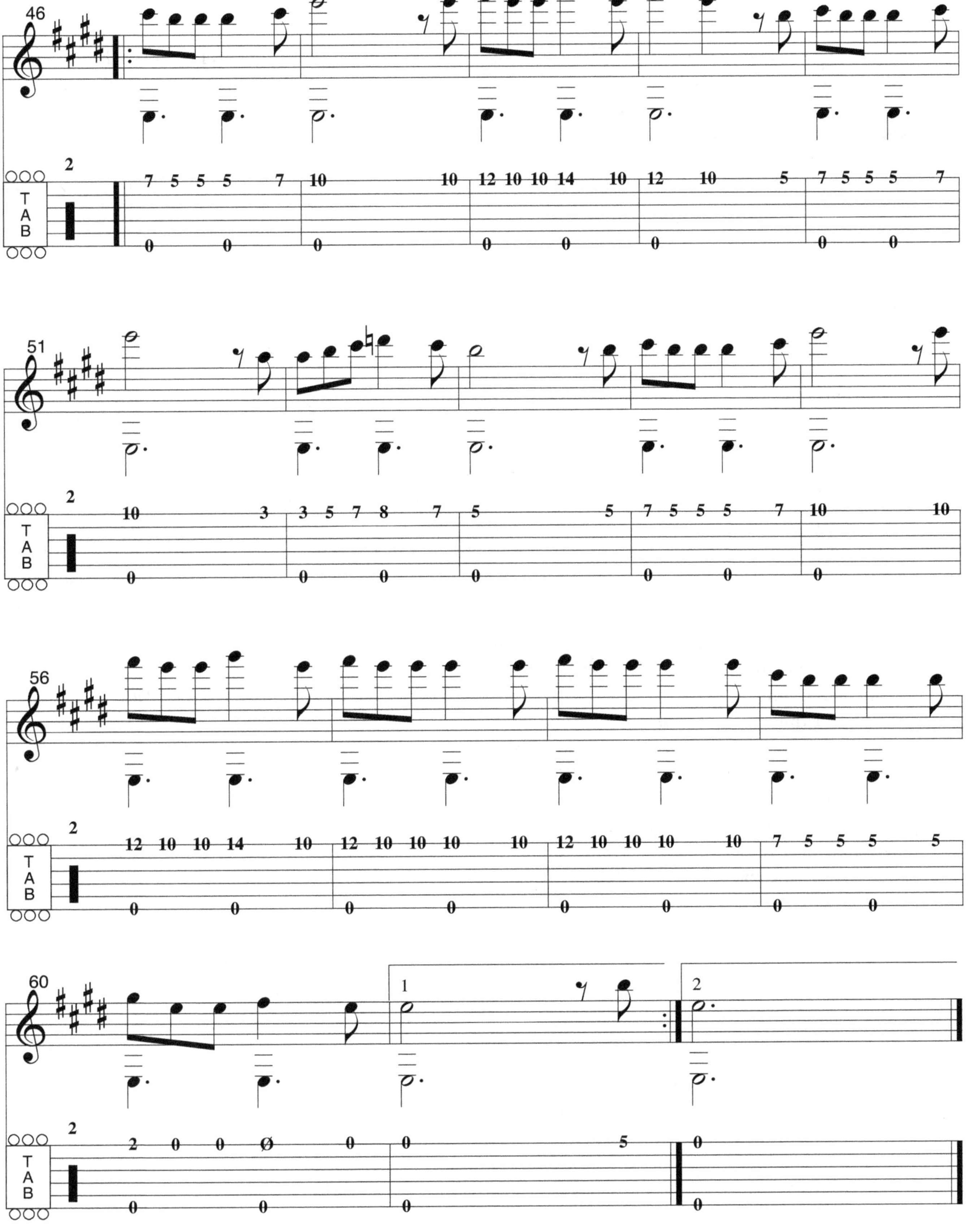
46
2
T
A
B
51
2
T
A
B
56
2
T
A
B
60
1
2
2
T
A
B

ABOUT "A WINDY GRAVE"

Not to overdo a good thing, but this is another piece that is played only on the high E string. It seems logical to include it here, and it is quite fun to play and entertaining to watch, because it uses both hands on the fretboard. It features some quite unusual crossed-hand passages where you fret, slide and pull off with fingers of both hands.

Like the *Highwire Hornpipe*, I recorded this piece on a 12-string, tuned to C# (3 frets low.) It also works fine on a 6-string, though it has a particularly Celtic sound when done on the paired strings on the 12-string. It really can't be done with fingerpicks, and even too much fingernail can get in the way.

Like the previous tune, it requires some left hand stretches, and you need to be able to hold a note at fret 5 with the 1st finger, hammer on fret 7 with the 2nd finger and then hammer on fret 10 with the 4th finger, while leaving the 1st finger still at fret 5. In fact, you play a triplet with frets 5, 7 and 10, and then play fret 12 with the index finger of the right hand, and trill it above the 4th finger of the left hand. This occurs first in measures 9 and 10.

I have used the classical guitar symbols *p-i-m-a* (Italian for thumb, index, middle & ring or annular) to indicate right hand digits. The h symbol above the staff is for a hammer-on, and a numeral above the staff is to indicate left hand fingers 1 through 4, because it is not at all obvious how to finger these passages. There is also a snowflake symbol above the TAB that indicates that the right index finger is hammering the note onto the fingerboard. This is known as 2-hand tapping, and using this technique to simulate a bagpipe is something I first worked out in 1984 when I wrote the epic *Minstrel's Dream*, a 23-minute long guitar solo.

In measure 25 the really tricky things happen. The high note on the 10th fret slides up from the 7th fret, fretted by the ring finger of the left hand. As you are sliding up, then the right hand crosses over the left hand and frets below it at the 5th fret for the last note of the measure, and after stopping at fret 10 to sound the note, the left hand then does a pull-off from the 10th fret down to the 5th fret, which is fretted by the right index finger. The right index finger then slides (there is an s above the staff to show this) up 2 frets to fret 7, and as it does, the left hand index finger crosses back over back to fret 2, and the right index finger pulls off its fret 7 note onto the fret 2 note being held by the left hand. This note is then hammered on to the 5th fret (by the 4th finger) and then the right index finger plays a triplet at the 7th fret that flows into a pull-off of the 5th fret to the 2nd fret, done with the left hand. It is worth doing an exercise where you plant the left index finger at fret 2, then hammer to fret 5 with the 4th finger, then hammer to fret 7 with the right index finger, then reverse this and pull off 7 to 5, then 5 to 2, all in a flowing motion. The key to making this style work is being able to make a plucked note, a hammered or pull-off note with either right or left hand sound the same volume, since they are mixed together in the same phrases in this piece.

*(Recorded on WP#104 **Of Wind & Water** in 1988.)*

A WINDY GRAVE

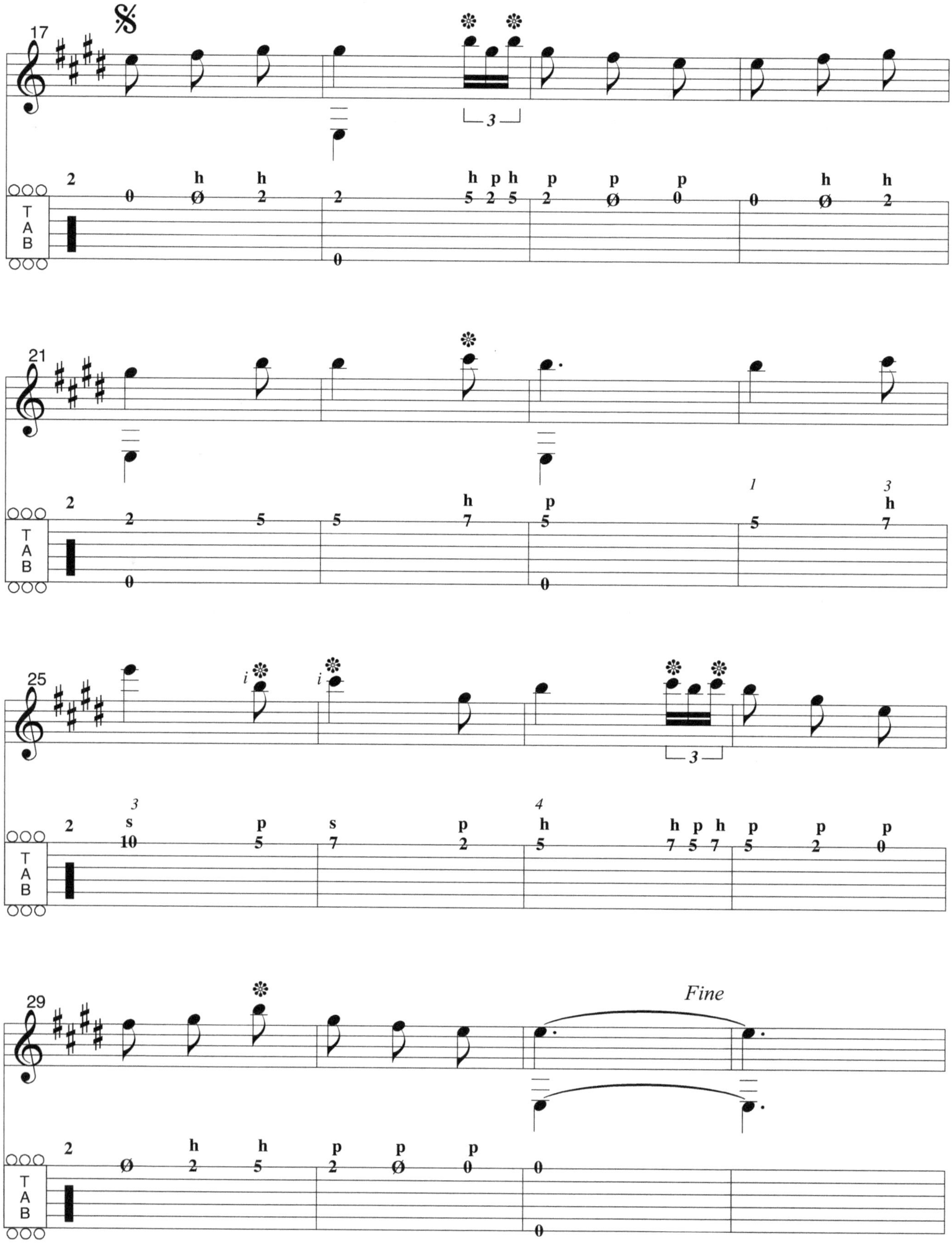
Fine

D.S. al Fine

15

HARD TIMES COME AGAIN NO MORE

by Stephen Foster Arrangement ©1994 by Harvey Reid (Quahog Music BMI)

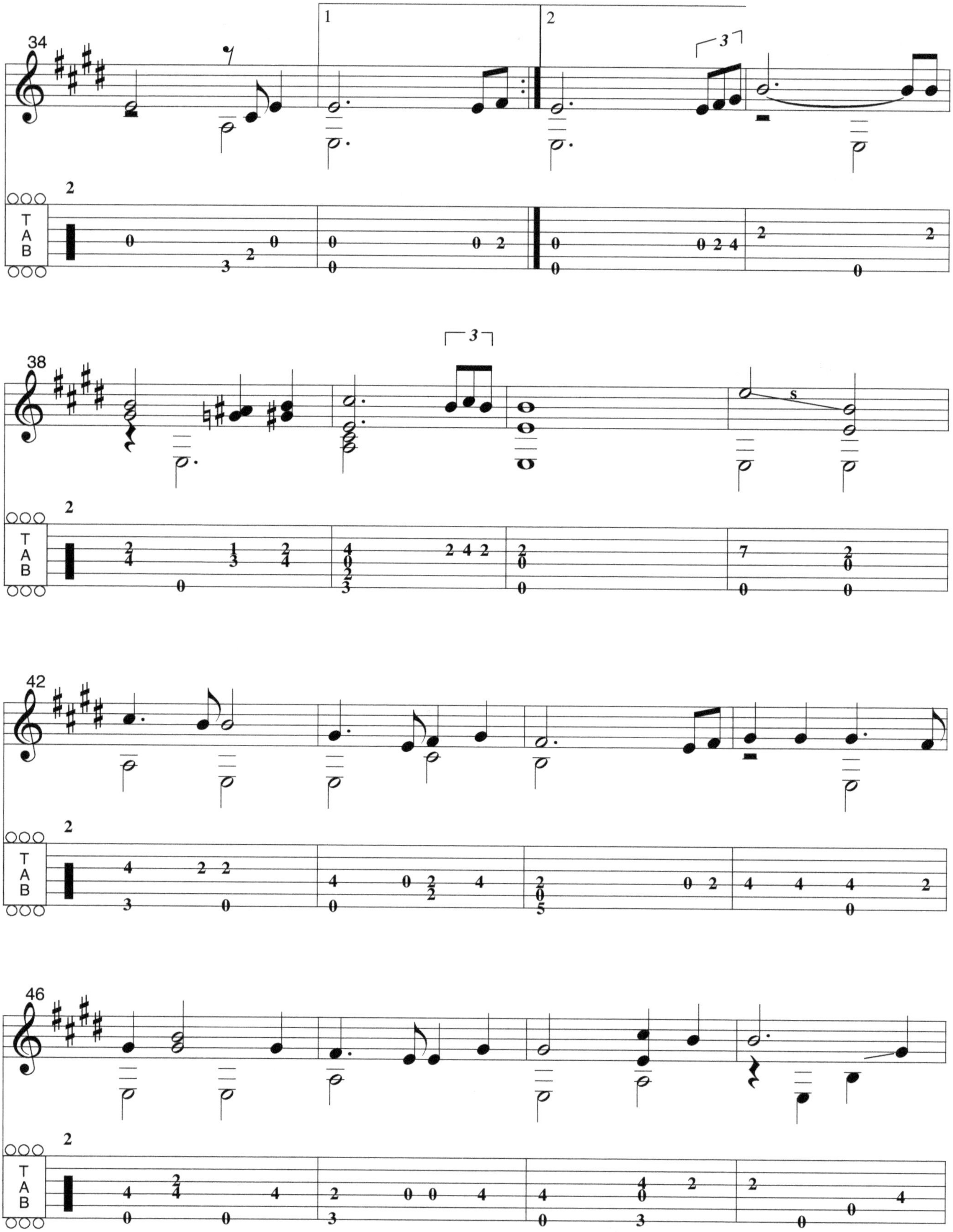
34
38
42
46
T
A
B

ABOUT "HARD TIMES (COME AGAIN NO MORE)"

This is not difficult, though it takes a 5-fret reach in measure 5. You also have to play a number of 4-fret reaches from the low E to the high E, and the piece is a good exercise for this kind of left hand work. I first recorded it on the 12-string with fingerpicks, but usually play it bare finger on the 6-string.

I also arpeggiate improvisationally quite a bit on the open strings during the sparser parts of the tune. This is easier to do when you are holding chords with the left hand, which is how I conceptualize playing it. In the opening phrase,

for example, I keep my 3rd finger on fret 2 of the G string while playing the melody phrase on the high E, and thus have a full 6-string tonic chord I can sweep or arpeggiate if I feel like it. During the parts mentioned above where the melody is on the high E and the bass lines are all on the low E, there are a lot of open strings in the middle you can hit if you feel like it, without interfering. When you finally land on the V chord in measure 17, I actually play the full V chord, x0220ø.

*(Recorded on WP#109 **Chestnuts** in 1994.)*

ABOUT "THE UNKNOWN SOLDIER"

I wrote this piece on the 6-string banjo (tuned the same as a guitar), but first recorded it on the guitar. It is played in G position in *Open A* capo configuration, and I play it bare finger, though I often use fingerpicks on other pieces. (On the 6-string banjo I play it with fingerpicks but no thumbpick, which is unusual.)

I always put a full capo on the 5th fret, then put the partial capo at the 7th fret, to give it the light, airy tone that I think suits the piece. My guitars have 14-fret necks plus a cutaway body, so if you can't reach the high notes on yours, drop the capos down a fret or two. With the capo 5 it comes out in the key of D, and makes a nice air to play as a duet with a fiddle.

In measures 5 and 24 I form these IV chords (actually C chord shapes) and the D7 & Em chords in measures 20 and 23, though in the TAB you only see part of these I fret the high notes in the Em section (measure 22) all with the 4th finger, and I like the slur when it slides down from fret 7 to 5 to 3. The hardest part in the piece is the stretch between the 3rd fret of the high E string and the ø on the bass E string. You really can't do this with a *Third Hand* partial capo.

*(Recorded on WP#108 **Circles** in 1992, then on WP#110 **Artistry of the 6-String Banjo** in 1994.)*

THE UNKNOWN SOLDIER

SUITE IN F (PART 1)

Esus

ABOUT "SUITE IN F: PART 1"

This is my first composition in *Esus*, equally flavored with the Celtic fiddle tunes and baroque music I was listening to at the time in 1982. It was the first piece to use the harp-like, cascading melody runs that *Esus* configuration allows. I use those scales heavily in Part 3 of this *Suite* (Parts 2 & 3 of the Suite are notated in the *Sleight of Hand* book.) and in Part 1 of the *Norway Suite* (Page 40). I finger a normal G chord in measure 7, and then jump to a partial "long" A chord (with TAB for the chord x0225x) In measure 10, just fret a barre Bm chord, which moves into a partial barre "long" A chord. I also often end with an extra note in the final chord, where I add fret 4 of the D string. This is my favorite inversion of a major chord, and it is not possible at all in standard tuning. 004700 is the spelling of the chord, or in scale numbers it is a 153100, and you can either play the high 2 strings or skip them and just finish with a 4-note chord with scale spelling 1531.

It is called *Suite in F* because I first recorded it in standard tuning with a full capo at fret 1 and then the Esus above it, which makes the piece brighter and sweeter. For convenience I usually just play it in E or Eb without the second capo, though it does sound better up high. I actually wrote it in G with a capo 3, which makes the left hand fingerings quite a bit easier, but the other parts of the *Suite* don't work as well up high, so it rarely gets played there except when I play it on 6-string banjo, where I sometimes capo 5 so it sounds in A.

(Originally recorded on WP#102 A Very Old Song LP in 1984, re-recorded in 1989 on WP#105 Solo Guitar Sketchbook and in 1994 on WP#110 Artistry of the 6-String Banjo.)

ABOUT "ARKANSAS TRAVELER"

All the other pieces in this book are for fingerstyle guitar, but I thought it would be acceptable to include this one I do with a flatpick. I think this arrangement allows enough open strings to ring that it makes it a strong solo flatpick piece, even by a fingerpicker's standards. There are a number of techniques that allow you to first play a conventional-sounding flatpicked fiddle tune, and then pull in more of the resonances, slurs, slides and open strings of the Esus configuration. Since the scale work is pretty normal feeling, you can almost forget that you have all those extra open strings to drone and weave in-between things. There are a lot of ø notes (same fret as the capo) on the high E string in this tune, and you can't do this with the *Third Hand* style universal capo.

On the recording, it is first played in the low octave, then two versions in the high octave, and then I do another high-octave variant that is sort of a dulcimer imitation, that is not shown here. Hold the pick very loose, and pluck the strings with the right hand up over the fingerboard to get a softer sound, and slur all the left-hand moves, keeping the fingers on the fingerboard as you move them. In this section (and also in the high octave section in measures 21 through 25), I plant the 3rd finger of the left hand at fret 2 of the G string and don't hit the low E or A strings if I can help it.

You can also make use of the open-tuned flavor to vary the sounds in the high octave. First I play it quite straight, with the scale notes on the high E string, then I play fewer melody notes on the E string and the B string next to it is droned. In measures 39-40 I drone the high E string and play the melody on the B string, which adds a different tone and flavor to the part.

In measures 45-48 I do a similar thing in the low octave, and play the melody by jumping up on just the D and A strings, while droning and crosspicking against the open B and high E strings. You can experiment and do some nifty arpeggiating this way, which also adds a nice contrast to the straight scale work in the low octave on page 1.

*(Recorded on WP#107 **Steel Drivin' Man** in 1992.)*

THE ARKANSAS TRAVELER

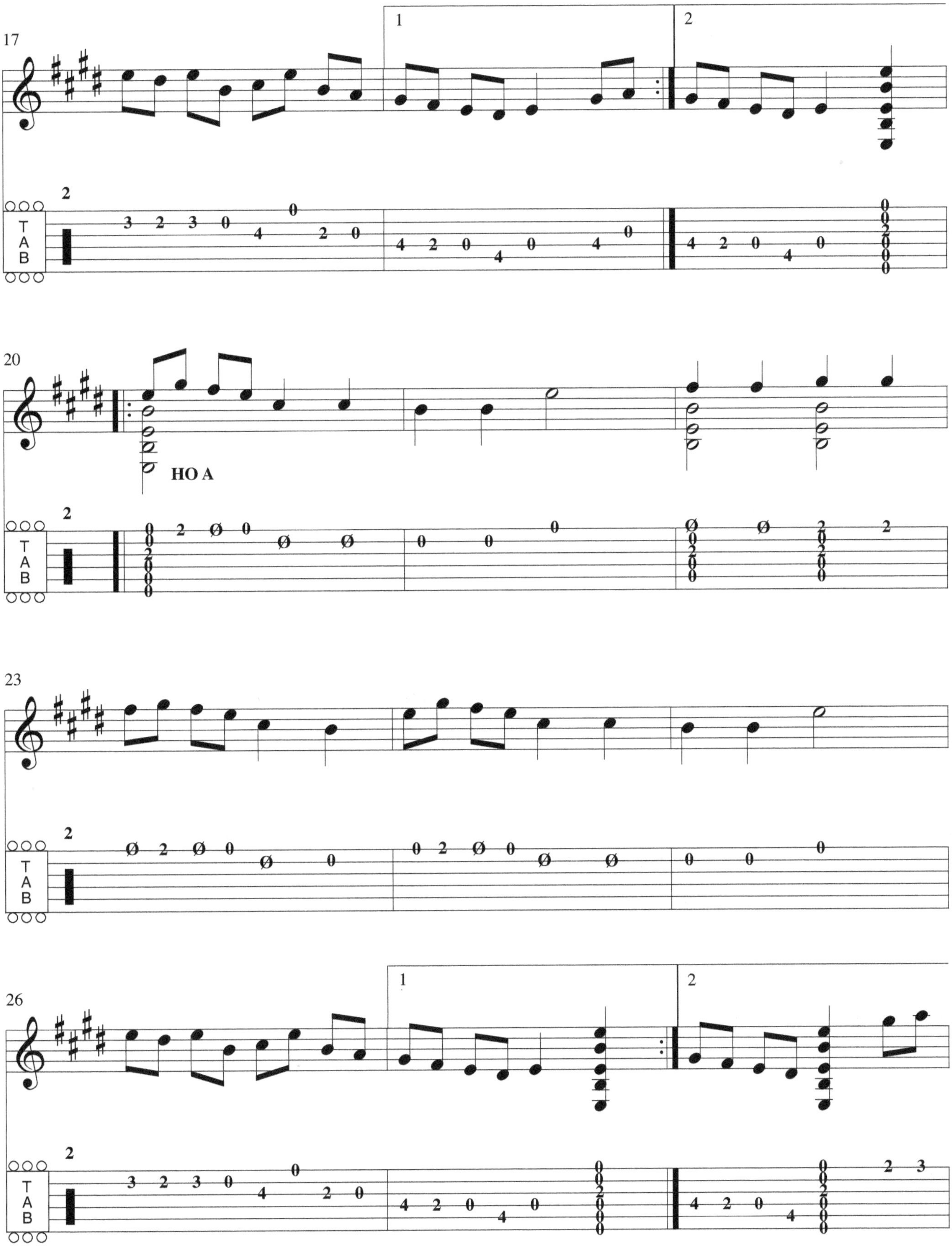
17
20
HO A
23
26

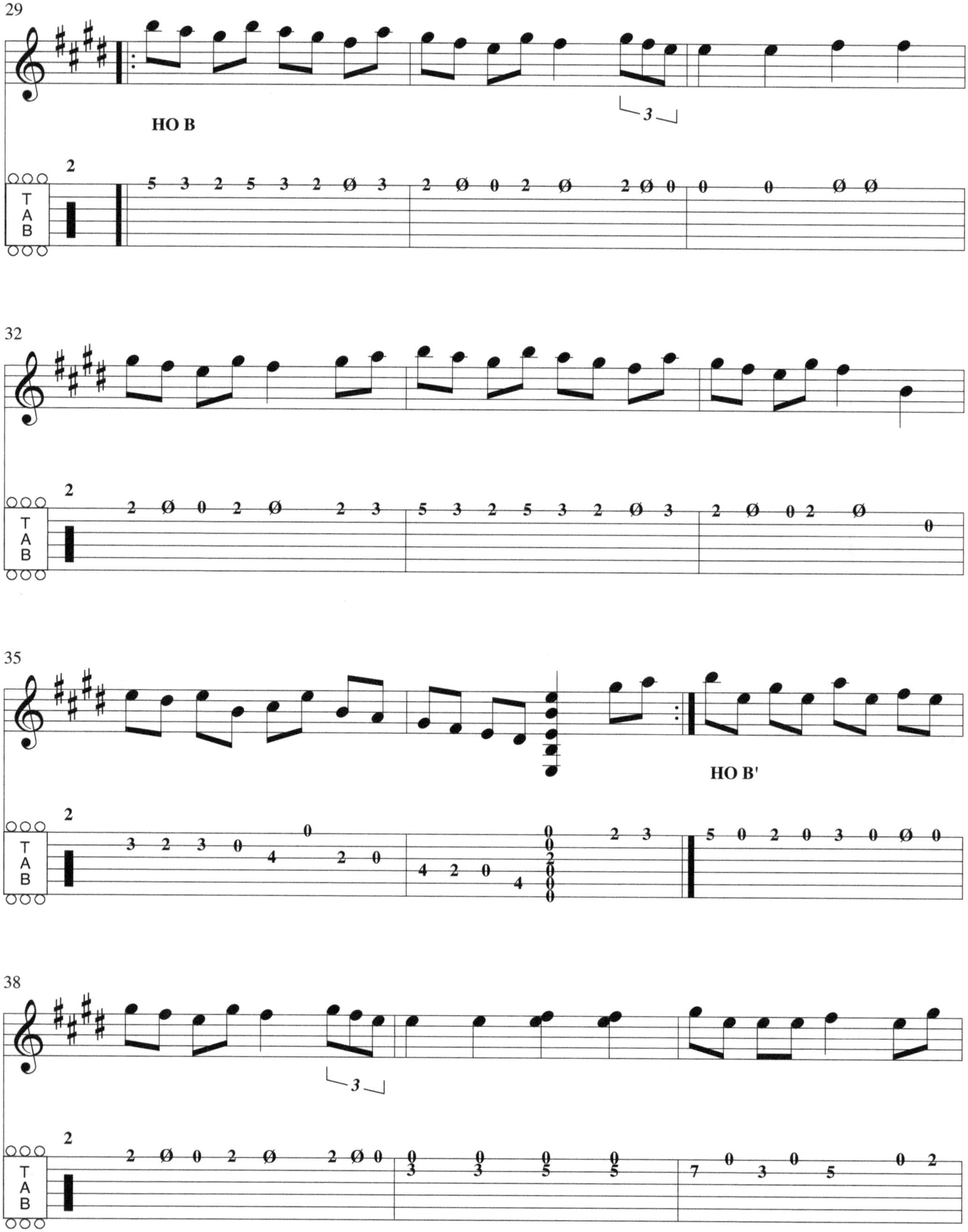
HO B
HO B'

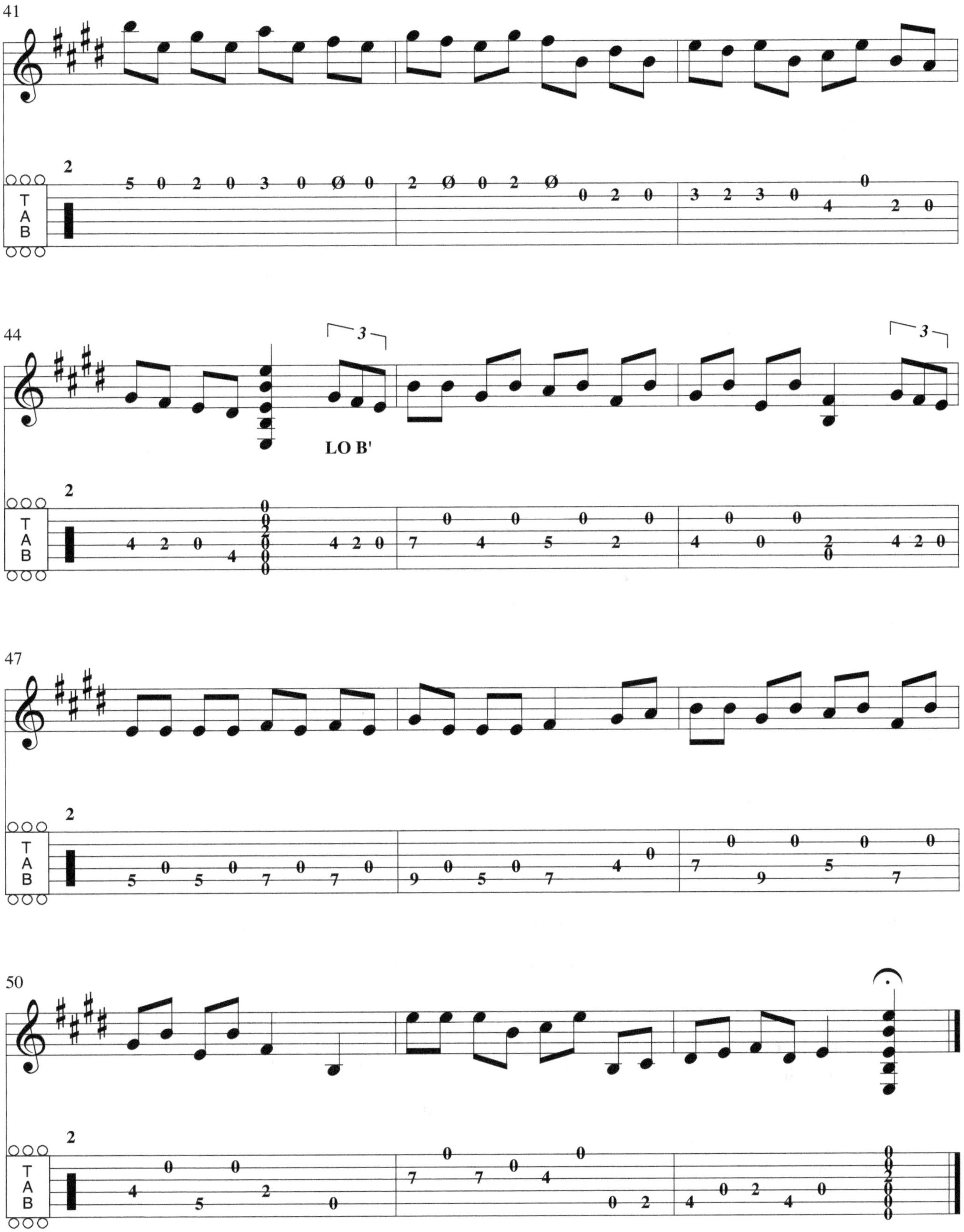
41
44
LO B'
47
50

ABOUT "THE MINSTREL BOY"

This is an arrangement of the classic Irish traditional song, and illustrates how you can play a majestic melody in Esus in 2 octaves, with rather independent moving bass lines. Only the low octave and high octave versions are shown here, though on the recording I do more variations since I play it more than twice through. This is sort of a composite of those, with a couple of the tricky bass lines shown. You really can't do things like this in DADGAD tuning, which most Irish guitarists use almost exclusively.

The B section (the chorus of the song, where the lyrics go *"Land of song, said the warrior bard..."*) of the song is only done in one octave, and it is easier than it looks. You just barre a Bm chord, and hold it through much of the section, with a quick jump to this E7 chord, where you reach over the capo to play the ø note, and then pull off to the open string and then jump back to the half barre A chord, then back to

the Bm and then a barre F# or F#7 which I usually play there. It's a really flowing way to get the melody to roll across the II7 chord change.

It suits the song to be able to play an open-string, ringing A part of the song, and then go into a strong, dramatic minor chord for the chorus, something you would struggle to do in DADGAD tuning.

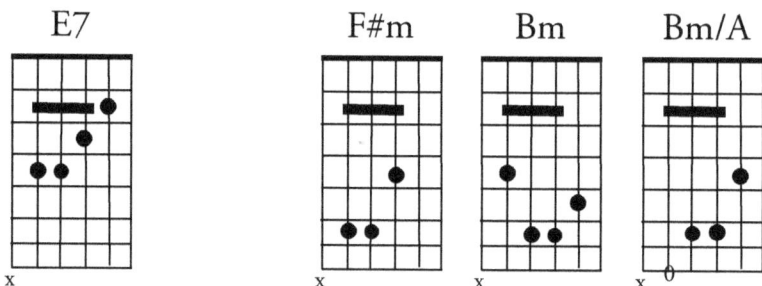

E7   F#m   Bm   Bm/A

<--These 3 chords I finger in quick succession in the low octave section in measure 33 for the last 3 beats, even though the TAB does not show much left hand action.

(Recorded on WP#109 Chestnuts in 1994.)

ABOUT "RED IN THE SKY"

This is both a slow jig and a requiem, written on Thanksgiving Day. I was listening to Bach's *Brandenberg Concertos* and dared to think I could set a similar mood. It evokes the counterpoint lines of classical guitar, while allowing the resonance of an open-tuned guitar. I think this is one of my best guitar pieces, and I am fond of the way it falls under the fingers, and the way it makes the guitar sound. In the opening measure, hold the D chord shown here, which moves into this A7 & then D in measures 2 and 3.

(Recorded on WP#108 Circles in 1993. A live version appeared in 1996 on WP#112 In Person.)

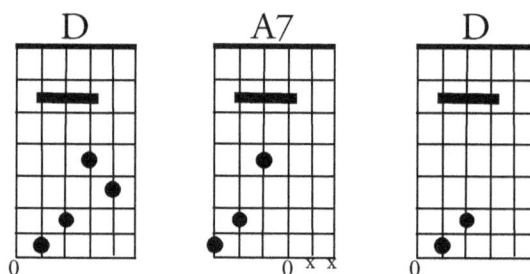

D   A7   D

THE MINSTREL BOY

Esus

29

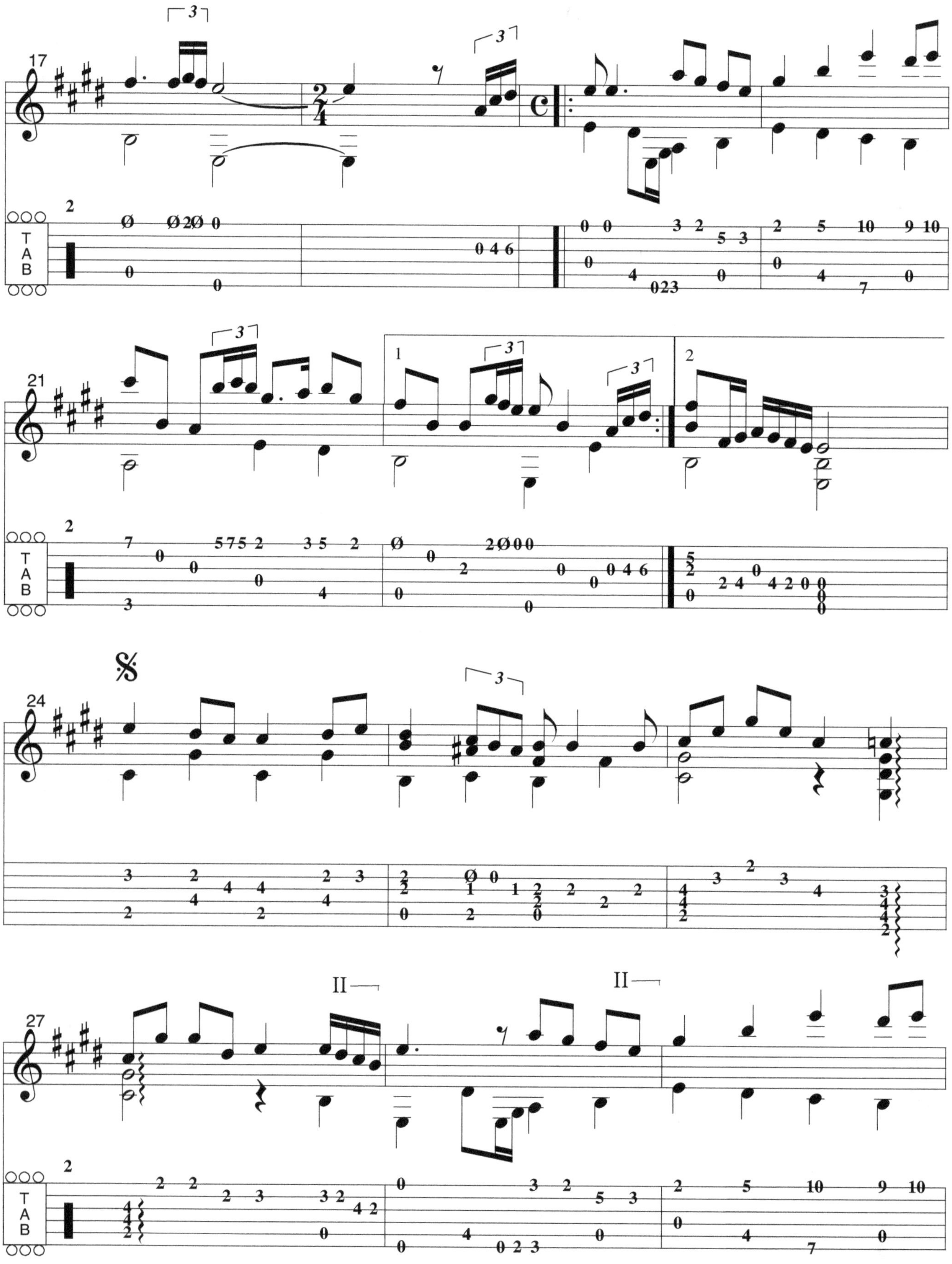
II
II

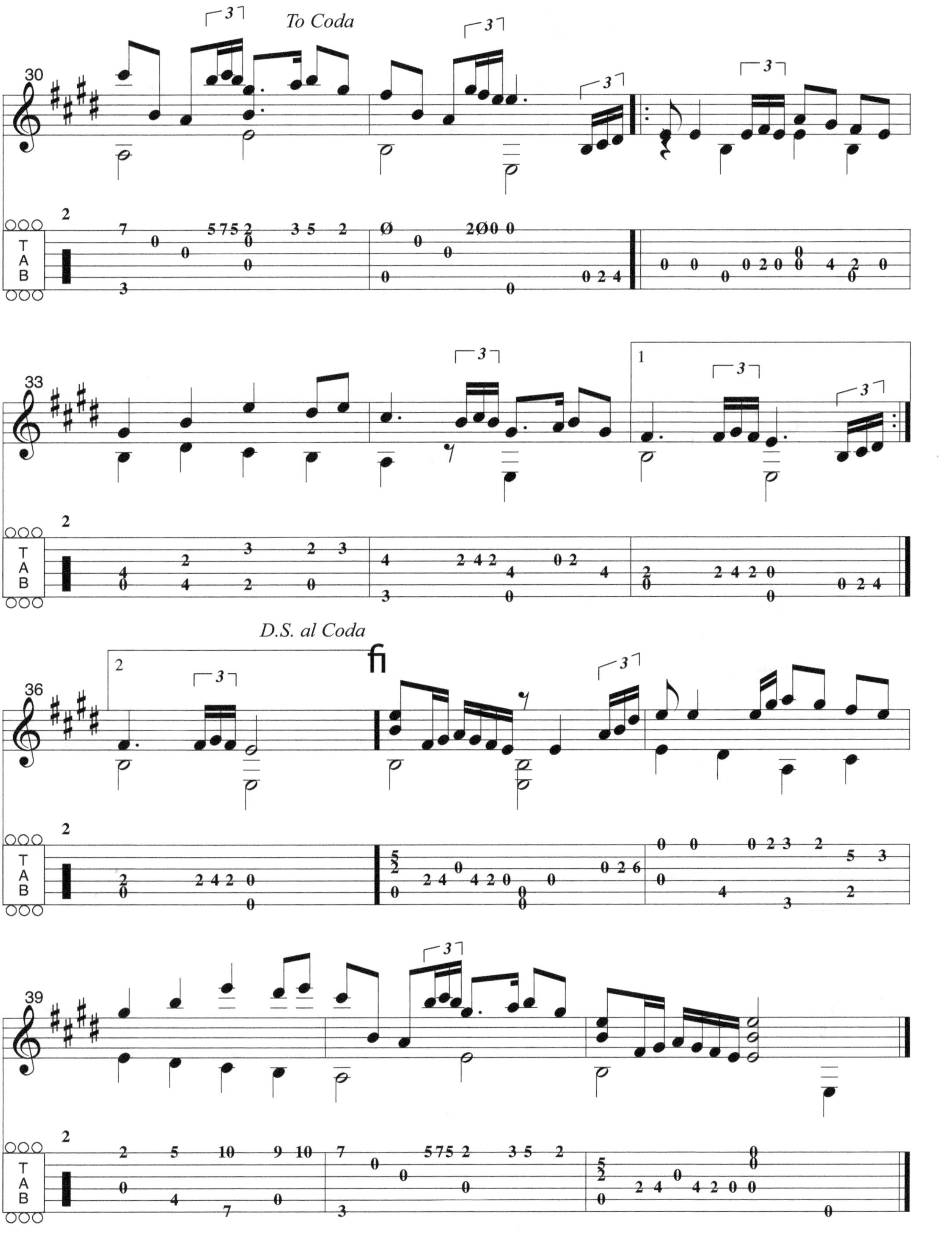
To Coda
D.S. al Coda
30
33
36
39
T
A
B

RED IN THE SKY

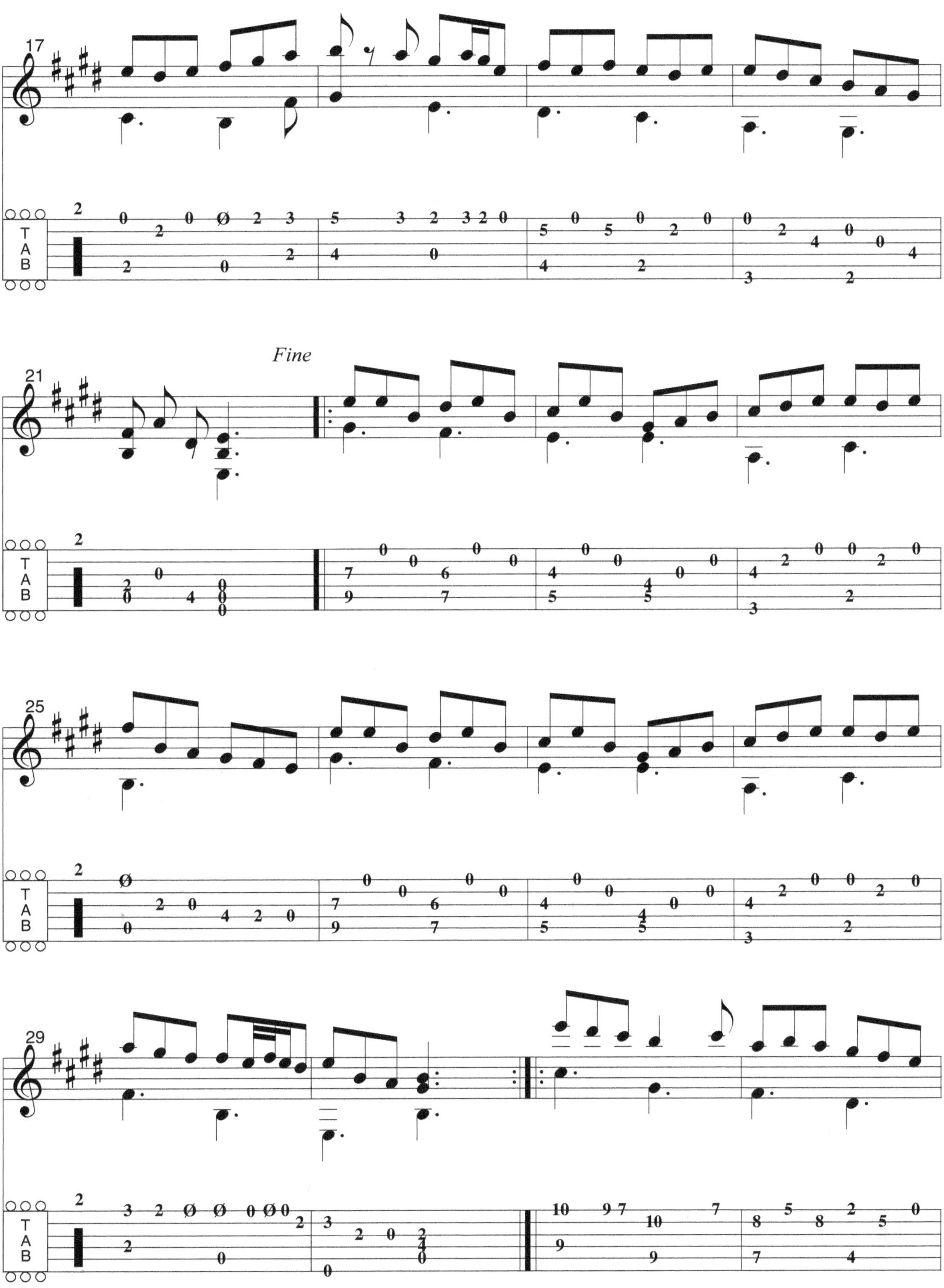
Fine

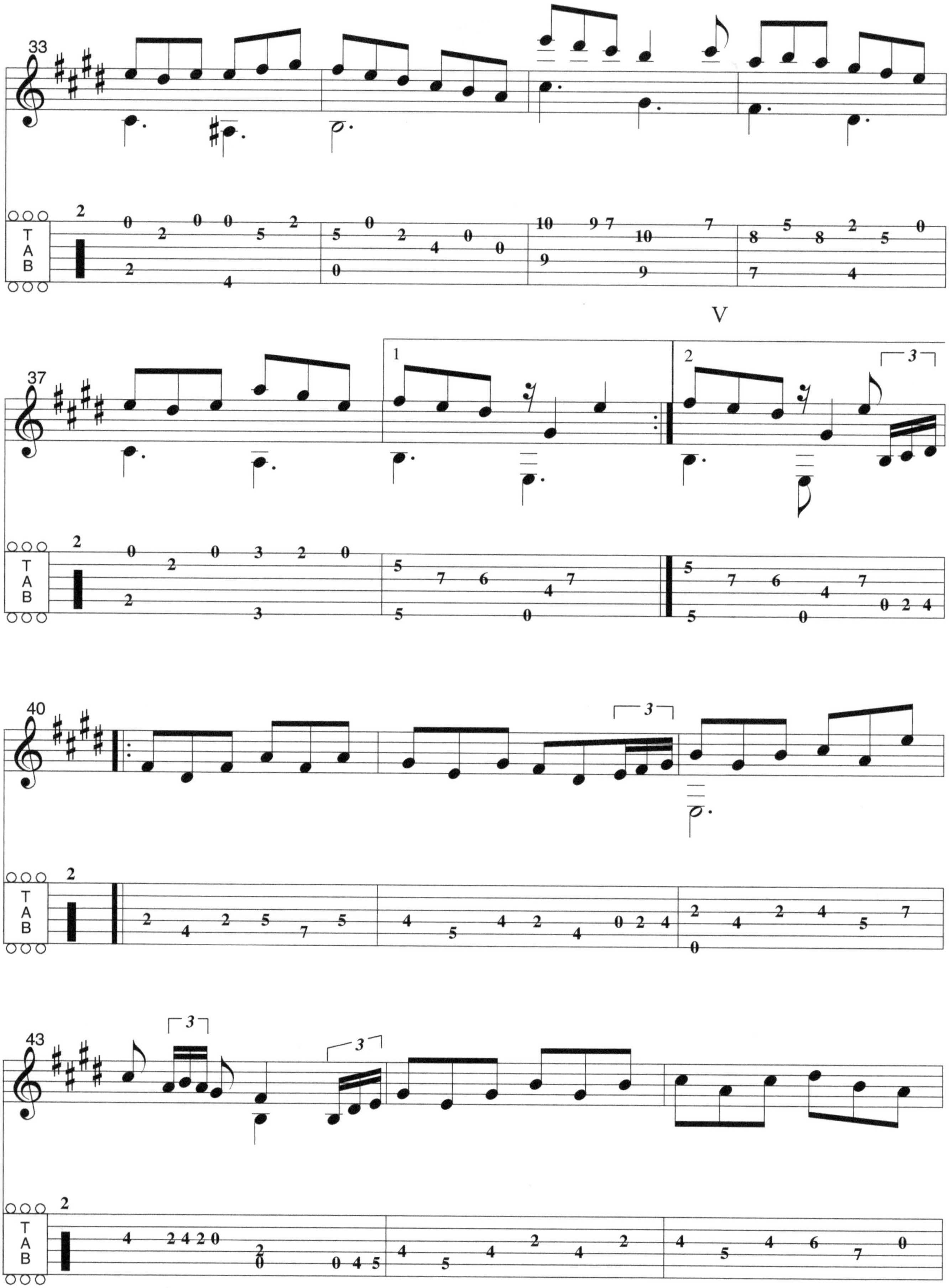

ABOUT "PRELUDE TO THE MINSTREL'S DREAM"

This was written in 1984 as the first section of a 23-minute, classical & Celtic guitar piece called *The Minstrel's Dream*, and was my first serious counterpoint *Esus* piece. It is still tricky to play, but the bass lines are quite satisfying and the effect of classical guitar with ringing open tuning-style tone is quite similar to *Red in the Sky*, which came 6 years later. Since this is a book of written guitar pieces, it makes sense to me to include both of them. These two pieces I consider to be strong evidence for the musical "validity" of the partial capo to the serious solo guitarist.

It is worth noting that in this and other baroque-style guitar pieces, it is quite common and usually desirable to play a bass note a little ahead of a treble note, even when they are on the same beat. (Actually the treble note is delayed a little behind the beat.) In the music, they are notated as if they are played at the same time, but the slight delay in execution allows the two notes to stand out, and is just a characteristic of this style of guitar playing, and something we do instinctively. Practice plucking a bass note with a treble note, and compare the sound when they are delayed and when they are not. It is an expressive and interpretive tool in your toolbox for this style of music, and probably not good to do it all the time.

Both this and *Red in the Sky* make very nice music for brunch, wedding ceremonies, and even Christmas concerts. The middle section is the hardest of the three parts in this piece. I always play both of these pieces without fingerpicks.

*(Recorded on WP#103 **The Coming of Winter** in 1986, re-recorded as a solo piece on WP#106 **Overview** in 1990.)*

35

PRELUDE TO "THE MINSTREL'S DREAM"

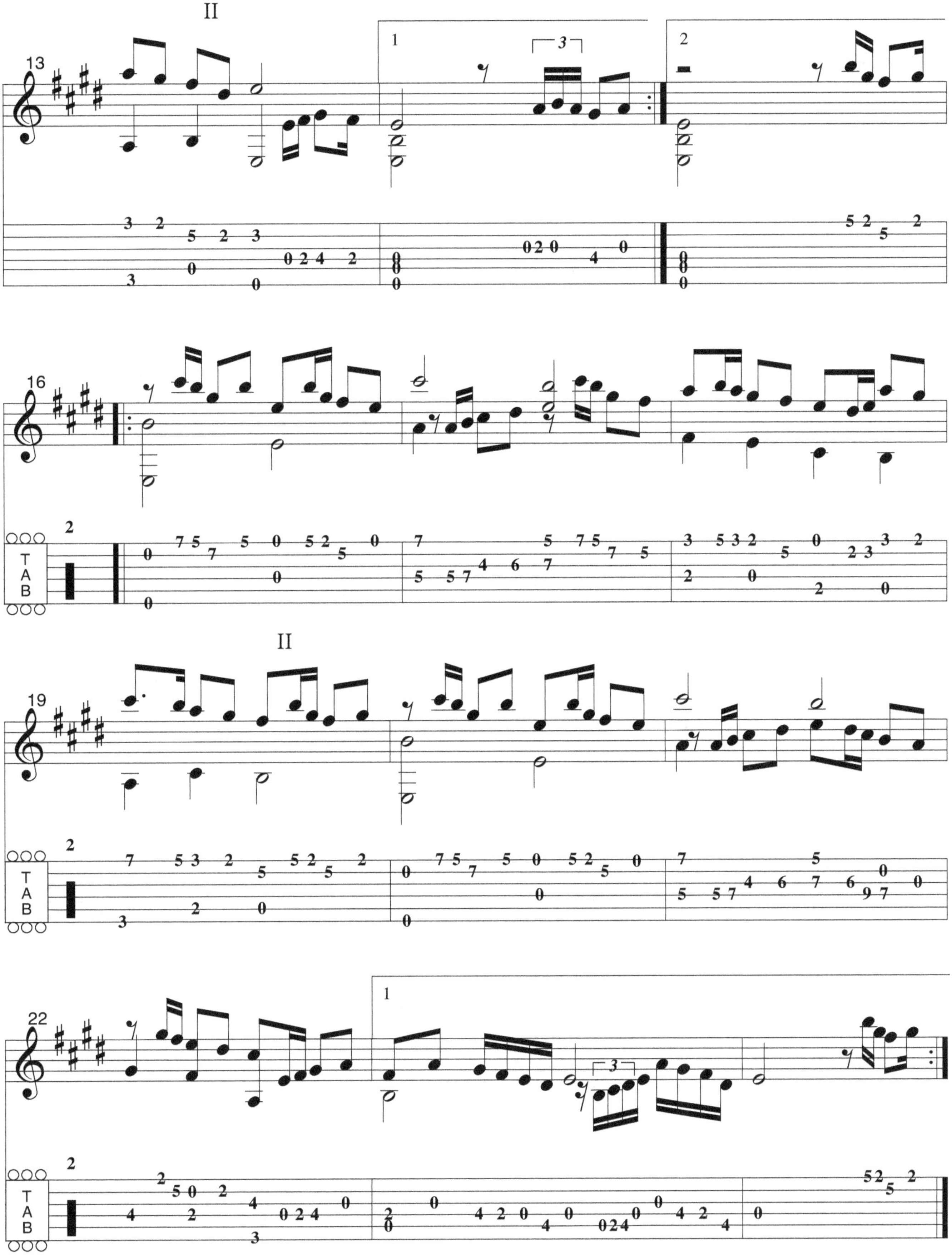
13
II
16
19
II
22
TAB

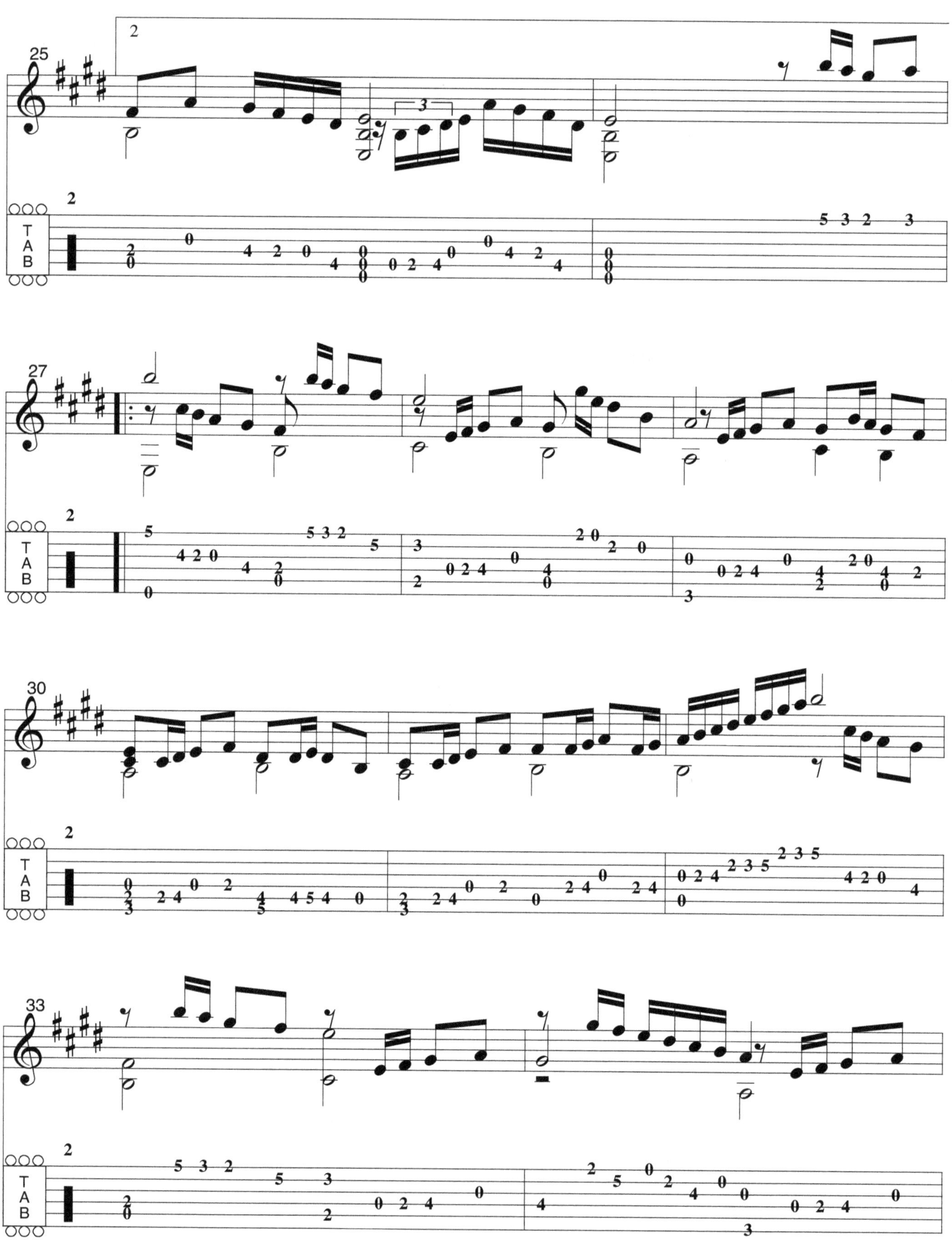
25
27
30
33
TAB

ABOUT "THE NORWAY SUITE"

This is the first serious composition for the *Asus* configuration. I had known about this tuning for 20 years, but had only worked up some fiddle tunes and always intended to spend more time with it. You put the capo on the 2nd fret to form the A chord, but tune the B string up to C. This creates a plaintive, suspended-4th chord ringing, similar to the Esus, but the melodies generally end up a string higher, so it is sweeter and brighter. I also put a straight capo on fret 2 or 3, which pushes the key up to C or C#, and the overall effect generates a bright and very lovely guitar tone.

Part 1 was inspired by Norwegian *Hardanger* fiddle music, and Part 2 is a slow Celtic air. I generally play this suite with fingerpicks, I guess because I like the extra "bite" and it sounds good played fast. Part 2 is relatively easy, and Part 1 is quite difficult. They probably should be separated in this book, but it makes sense to keep them together.

When you use the *Open A* or the *Asus* capo configurations, you generally play in G position to sound in A. Part 2 is a slow modal air in G position, but Part 1 of the *Norway Suite* is actually played in what would be C position. Its cascading melody lines are possible because you no longer need 3 fingers to fret the C chord, since the B string is a half step sharp. Only the bottom 2 fingers are needed, leaving the others to work the melody lines against the bass notes. It's possible to roll the flowing melody notes through I, IV and V chords, and it keeps its fullness. The effect of the flowing melody lines is better than any such thing I have ever found on the guitar. It has a ringing quality and the suspended tuning adds a plaintive feeling, and these remind me of the droning and flowing *Hardanger* fiddle.

*(Recorded on WP#114 **Guitar Voyages** in 2000.)*

NORWAY SUITE: PART 1

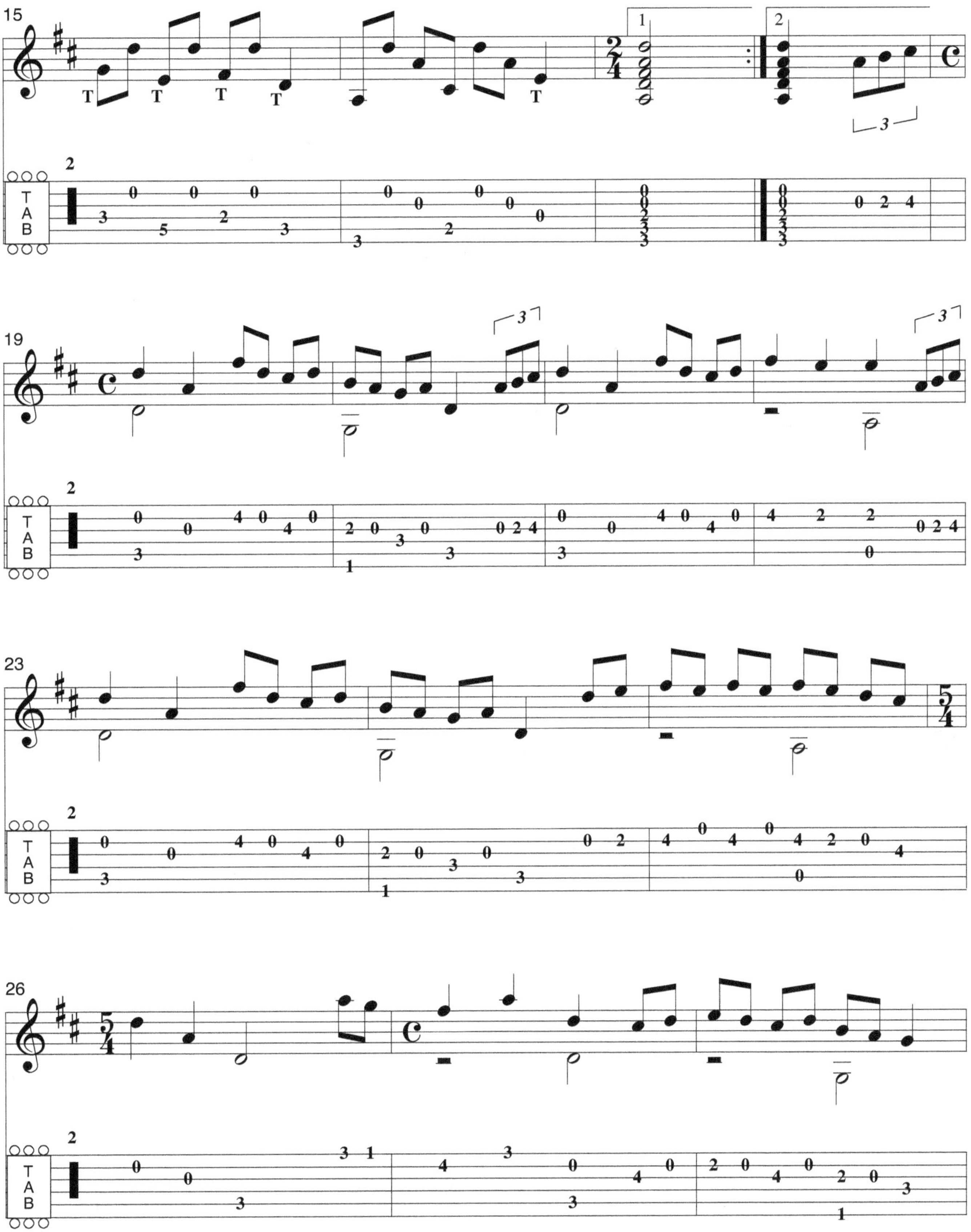
15
T T T T T
1
2
3
19
3
3
23
26
TAB

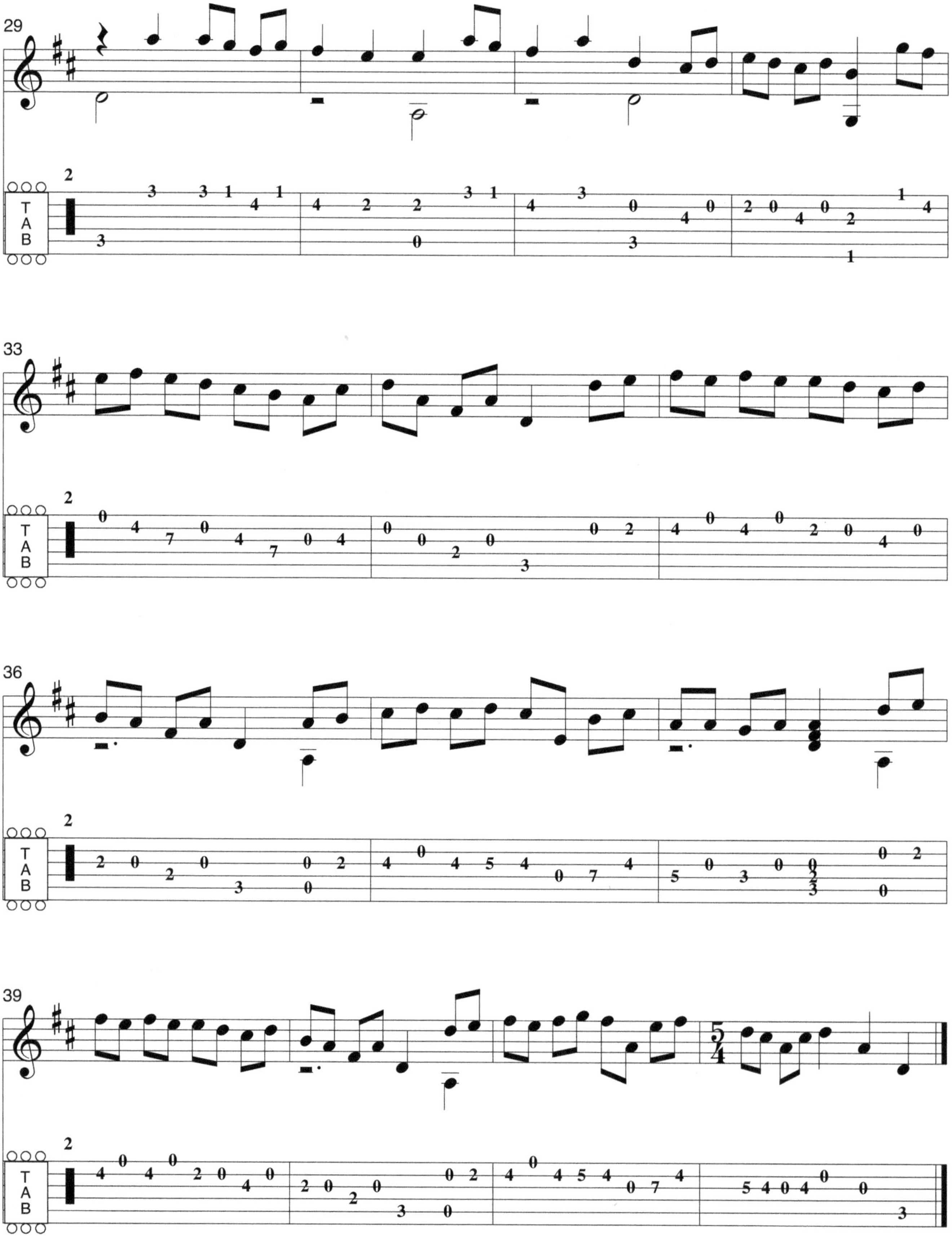
29
2
T
A
B
33
2
T
A
B
36
2
T
A
B
39
2
T
A
B

NORWAY SUITE: PART 2

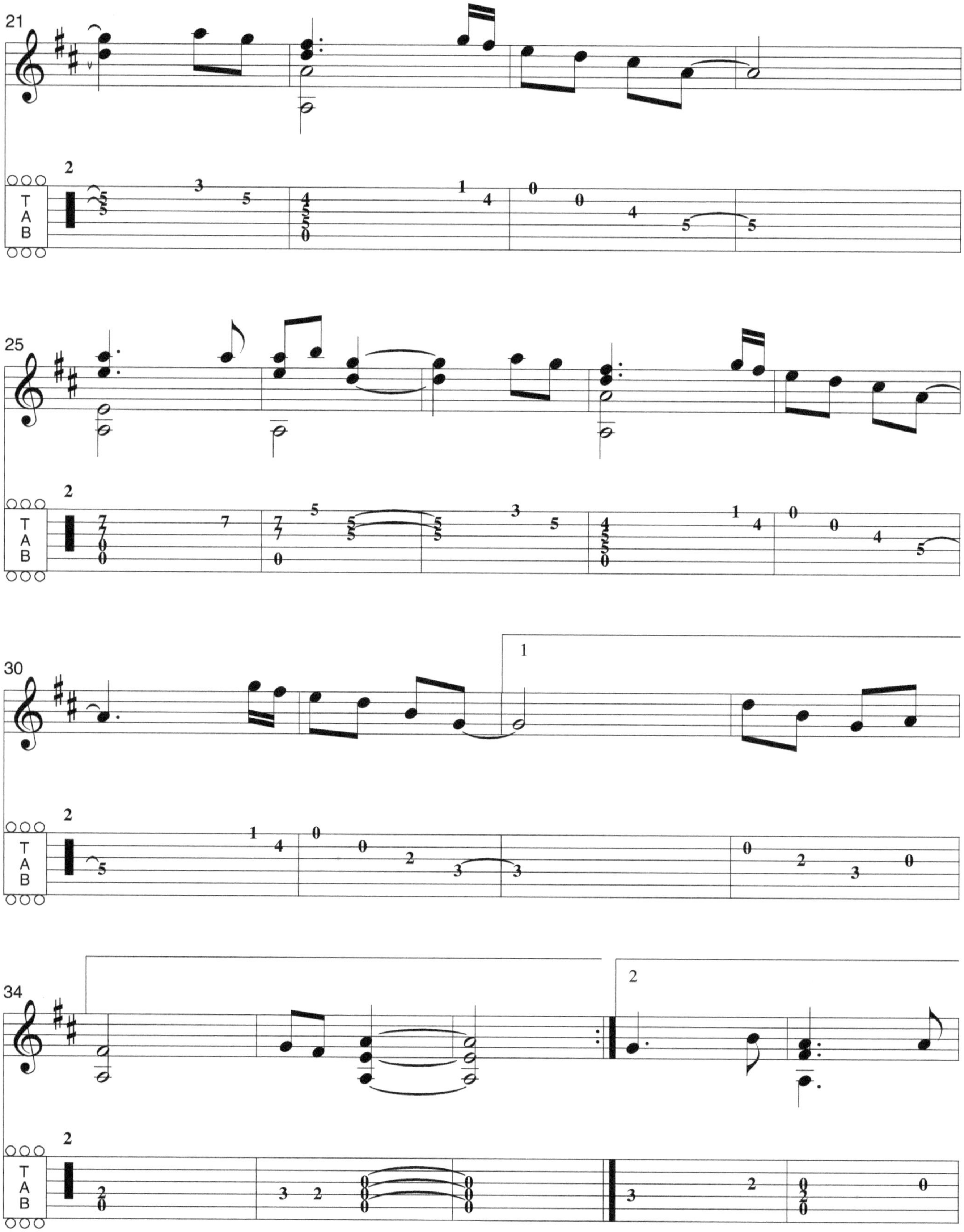
21
25
30
1
34
2

ABOUT "THE STAR ISLAND JIG"

This one started out as a fiddle tune played in a jig tempo but took on a life of its own, and I don't think it would even sound that good on a fiddle. But it has a lot of drive, and is one of the best examples I can present to show how the *Esus* configuration allows a powerful, ringing drone rhythm and bass notes, with fast and flowing melody notes played against it. The rhythmic drone is at the heart of a lot of folk musics, and the scale work really benefits from the ringing open bass strings. I originally recorded this and wrote it on the 12-string, but re-did it in 2002 on the 6-string, tuned to Eb, which is what is on the 2nd recording I did of this. I play it with fingerpicks, and it's always a thrill and a challenge.

The opening 2 sections are almost all played on the high E string, except for the 1st fret flat 7 note on the B string. I often play different bass notes and more of them than is shown here- this is the stripped-down version. The TAB here often shows just the low E string being played, but there are 3 open bass notes to choose from, and I do different things depending on how I feel. Sometimes it's nice to drone the 4th string tonic note for a while, which is an octave higher than the open low E, and then it makes it somewhat dramatic when you kick the bass E string back in.

To some degree in this piece I also do the Merle Travis-style muting of the bass strings with the heel of the right hand, and I sometimes also physically hit the same area of the strings where I am muting with the heel of my hand at the same time I pluck the strings, to make both the muted bass sound and a percussive thump. On stage, plugged in, this really shows up and adds to the rhythmic drive. Guitar tops are pretty tough, and you'd be surprised how hard you can hit them.

There are not a lot of chord shapes held down in this piece (unlike *Macallan's Jig*) and for the most part it is scale work played against a drone bass. I probably should have specified more clues as to the left hand fingering in the trickier passages. In measures 87-90 & 97-100 I hold the 3rd fret G of the bass string for the IV chord, then hold the 2nd fret A of the G string for measures 103-104. When the song modulates to A in measure 111, I hold down the x0220ø (V chord) for quite a while, leaving the 4th finger free, and the 3rd finger stays on fret 2 of the G string (measure 119) as it moves into the D chord.

(Recorded on 12-string on WP#108 **Circles** *in 1990, re-recorded on 6-string* **Seacoast Guitarists Vol 1** *in 2002, then it appeared in 2004 on the concert DVD* **One April Night** *.)*

THE STAR ISLAND JIG

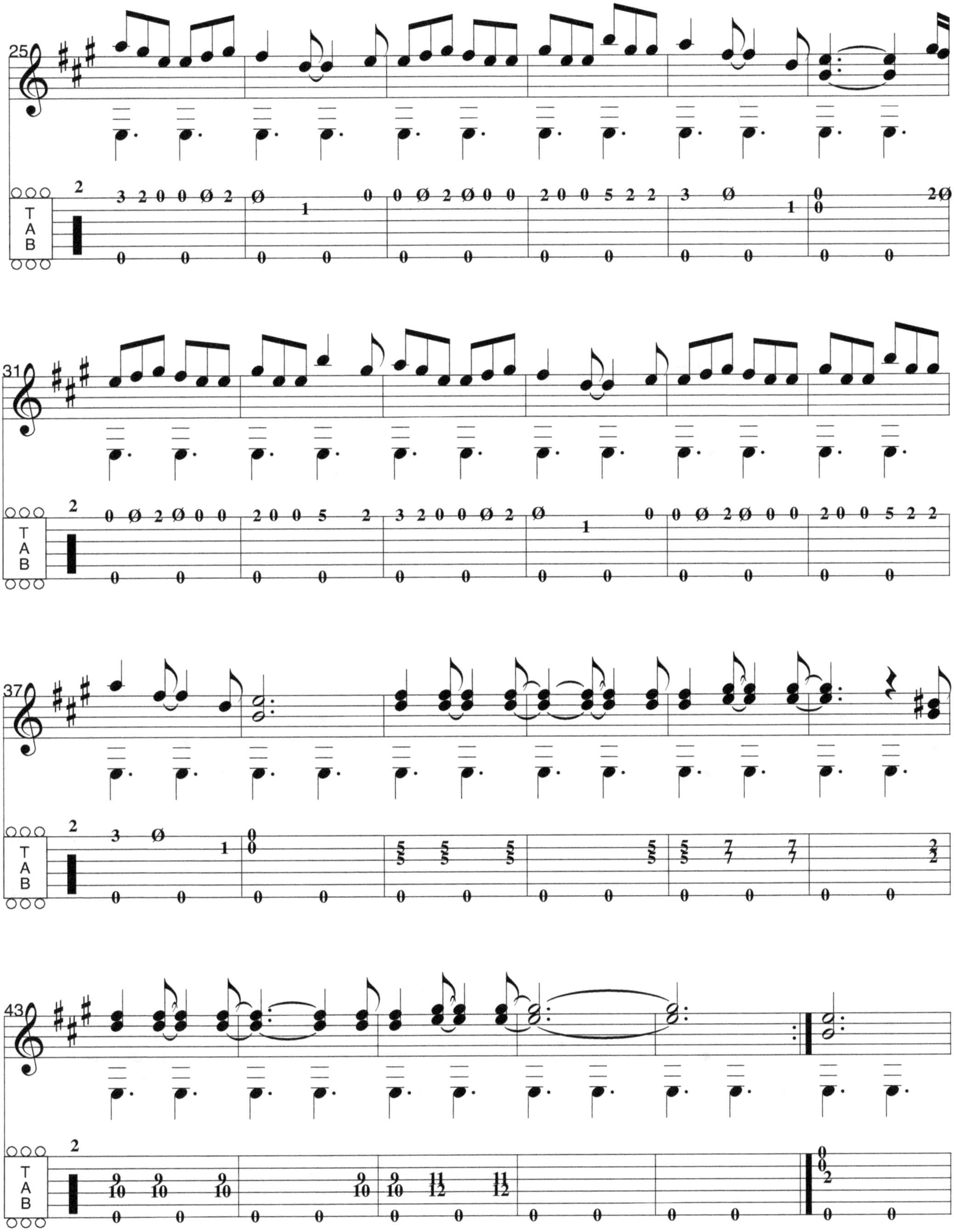
25
TAB
31
TAB
37
TAB
43
TAB

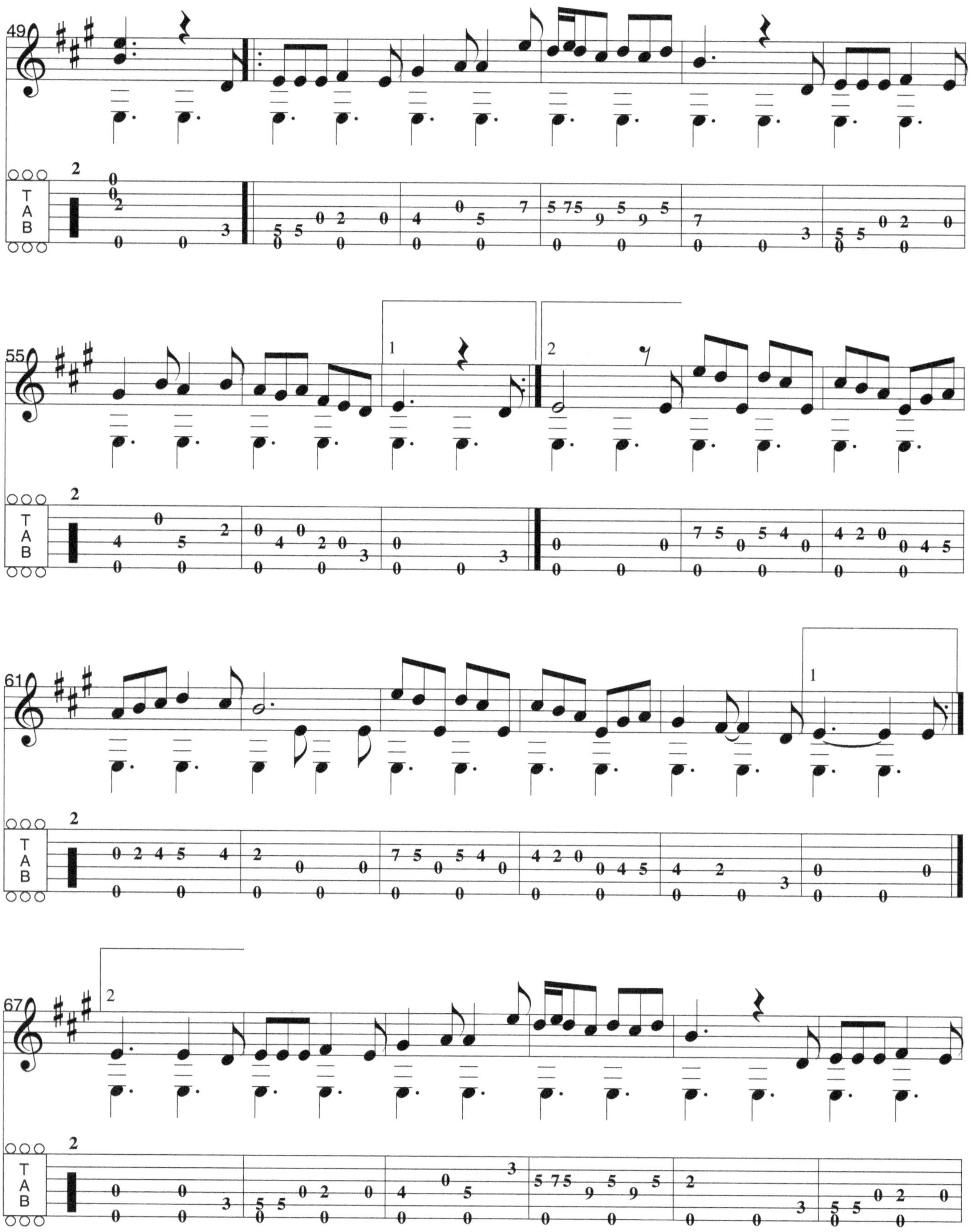
49
TAB
55
1
2
TAB
61
1
TAB
67
2
TAB

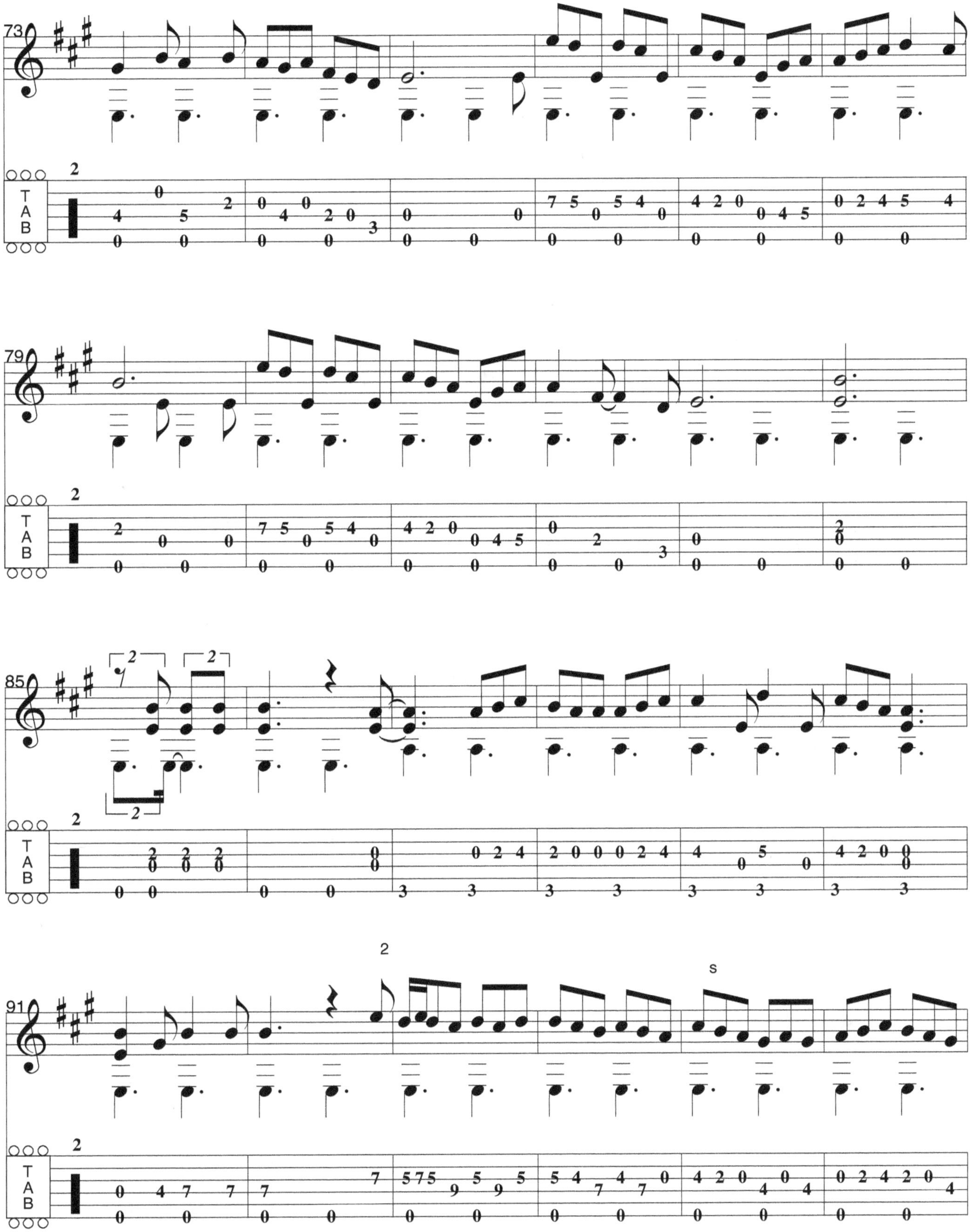
73
79
85
91
TAB

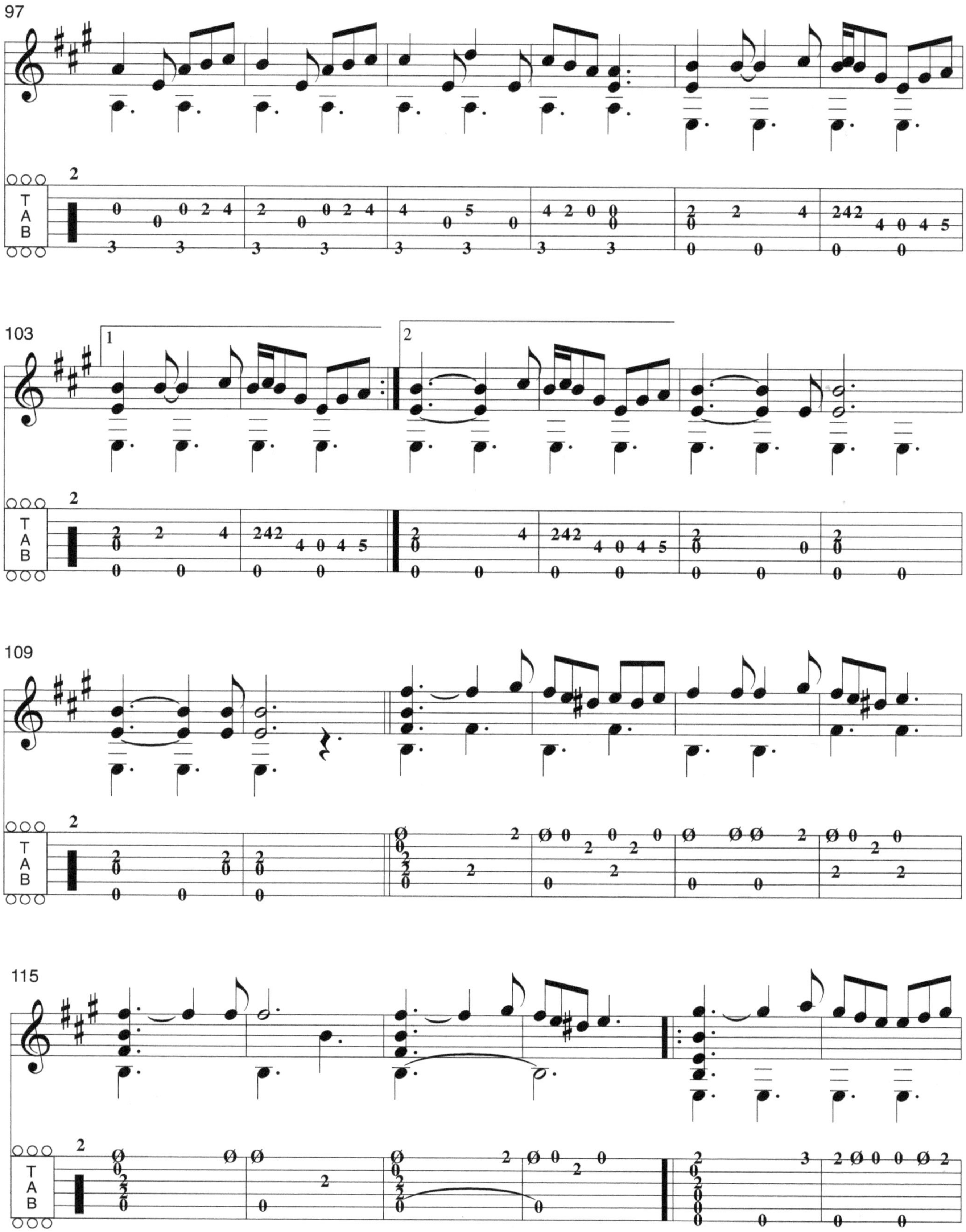
97
103
1
2
109
115
TAB

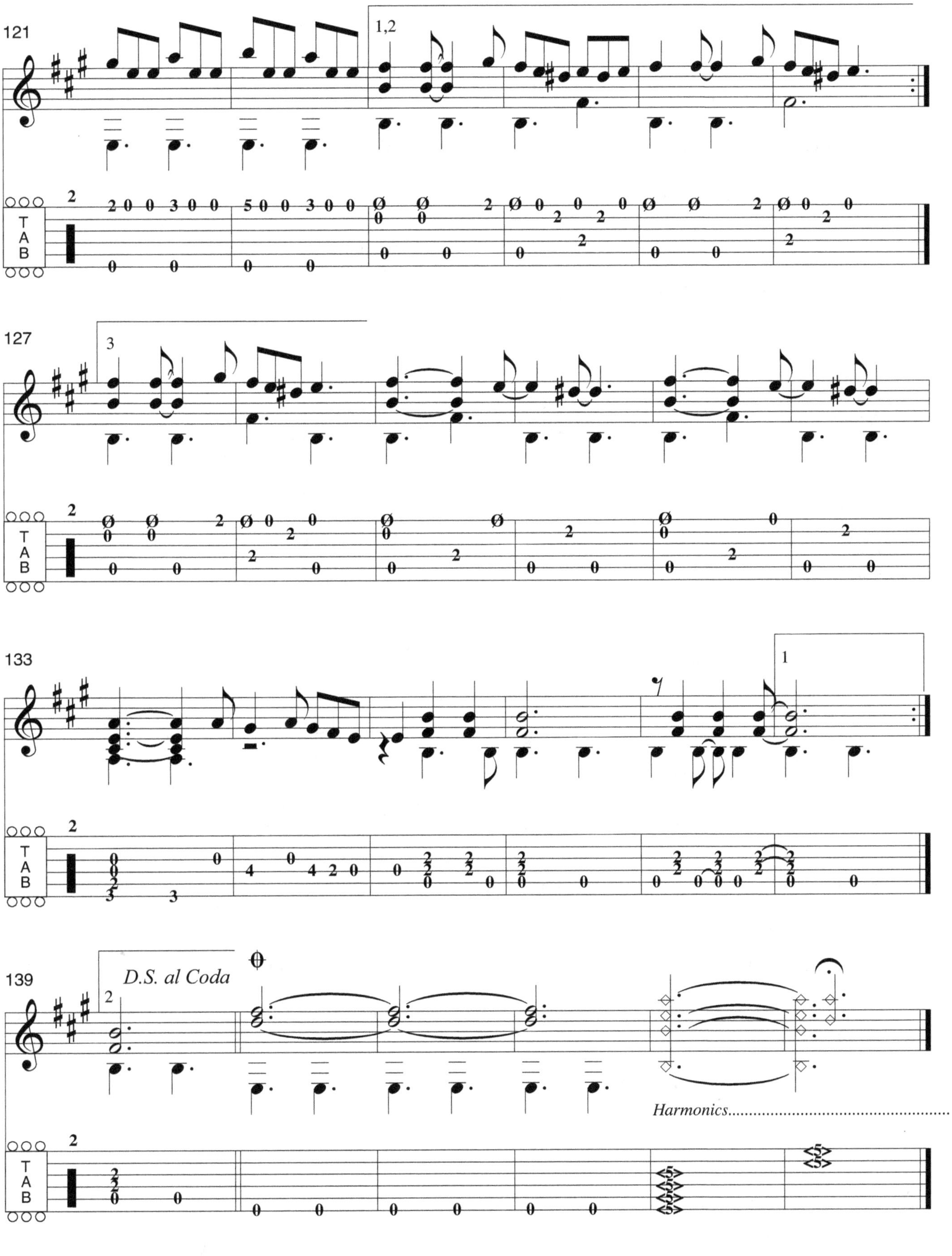
121
1,2
127
3
133
1
139
2
D.S. al Coda
Harmonics

ABOUT "MACALLAN'S JIG"

I have written and recorded 3 other *Esus* jigs (*Daybreak in Dublin, Scotland Suite-Part III, The Gaoler's Jig* and *Racing the Storm*) in addition to the two that are in this book: *Star Island Jig* and *Macallan's Jig*. This one is probably the most involved and the most difficult of the five. It was written and recorded the night before the album went to mastering, and over the course of playing it for years, it has evolved a little, and not everything on the recording is shown exactly here. I also don't play the parts in exactly the same order as the recording- when I finish Part 5 in measure 88 now I just play the opening lick of Part 1 and end it, though on the recording, I must have been over-caffeinated because I play through Part 2 also there and then repeat Part 1 again instead of ending it. It has 5 sections, 4 of which are fiddle tunes in AABB structure, (Part 3 is half a fiddle tune) and it requires some pretty strenuous left-hand and right-hand work, and a lot of stamina to keep it going forward. The opening lick requires a pretty athletic 4th finger on the left hand, and the last chord in the B part of Part 1 is a partial barre 0077xx, though it's perfectly OK to just play the simple I chord- 000200 and rest for a second.

Use this D chord at right-->
for the opening and closing
strummed rhythm chord,
and for measures 1 & 2,
hold the 1st finger in place
and just shift it across to the
4th string for measure 4.
The 3rd and 4th fingers do
all the work in Part 1.

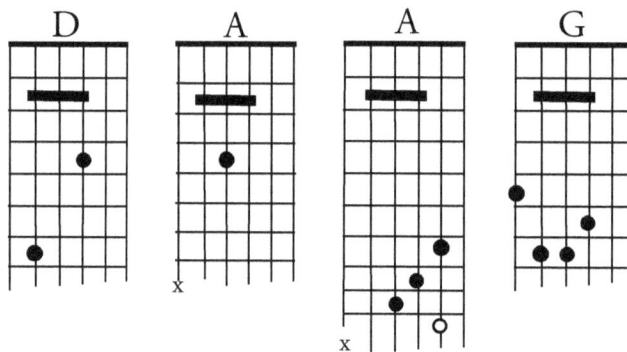

D   A   A   G

<--This G and A chord
(left) are vital for this
piece. They first appear in
measures 11 & 12 and the
4th finger pulls of the A7
at fret 8 of the B string to
end Part 1.

Use these first -->
two G and D7
chords at right for
Part 4 (measure
55) where it
modulates into G.

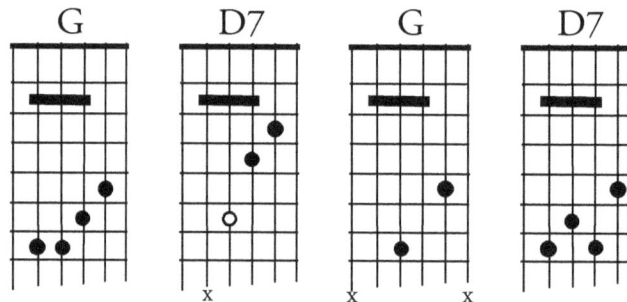

G   D7   G   D7

<-- Hold these
positions for 2nd
set of G and D7
chords for the B
part of Part 4
(measures 65-66)

Measures 46 and 47 are just barre Bm and G chords in the bridge, which is Part 3.

In the A part of Part 5, measure 82 , slide the 7th fret to the 10th fret with the 4th finger.

I don't really expect a lot of people to be able to play this, but it is really fun and quite exciting to play, and a great illustration of what is possible in this configuration in the manner of a fingerpicked fiddle tune with a lot of rhythmic drive. It shows that a solo guitar can play Celtic-style fiddle tunes without another rhythm instrument. In fact, if you learn this one I'll buy a ticket to see you play it.

*(Recorded on **Fruit on the Vine** in 1998.)*

MACALLAN'S JIG

Esus

1 | *2* Fine

Part 2

53

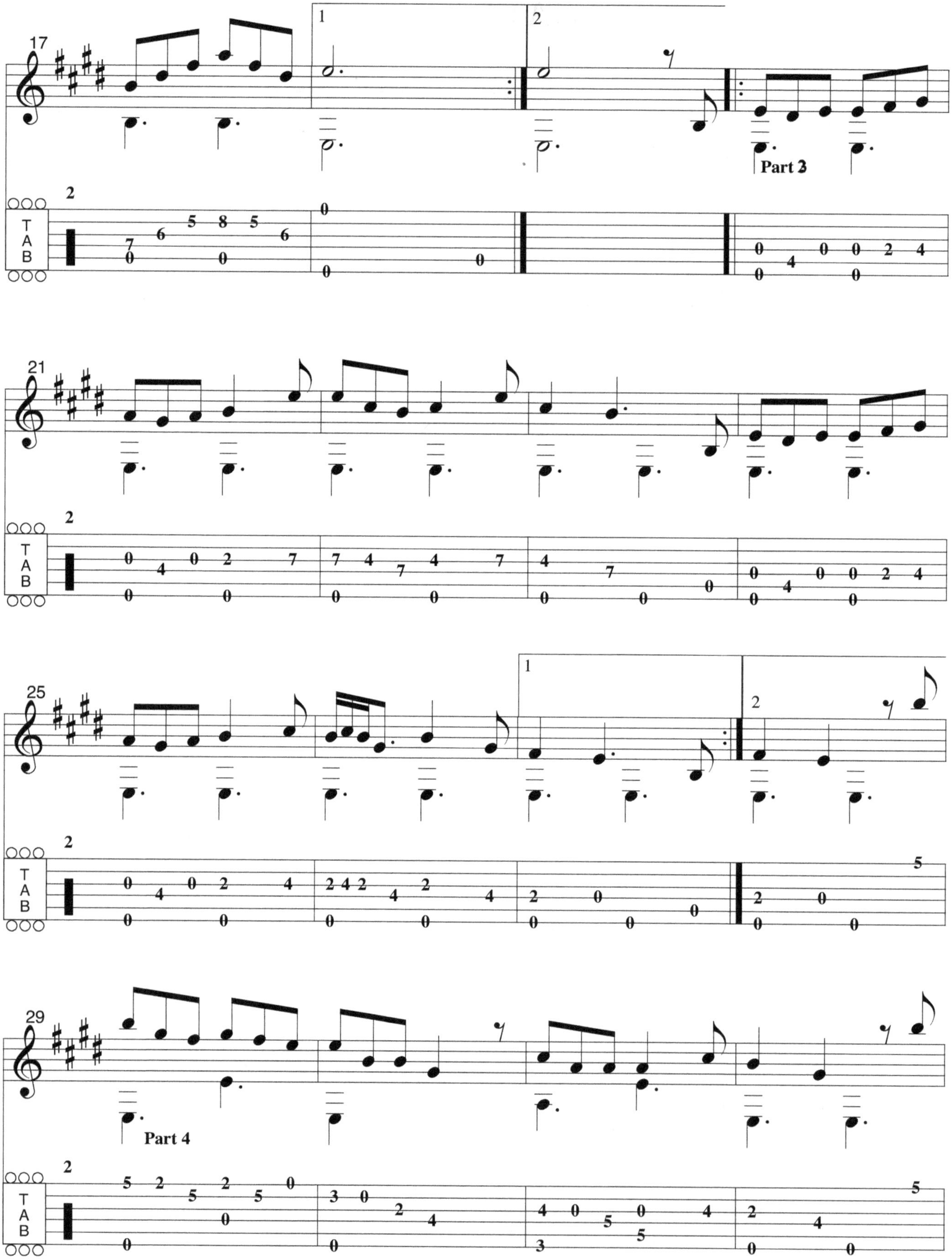
Part 3
Part 4

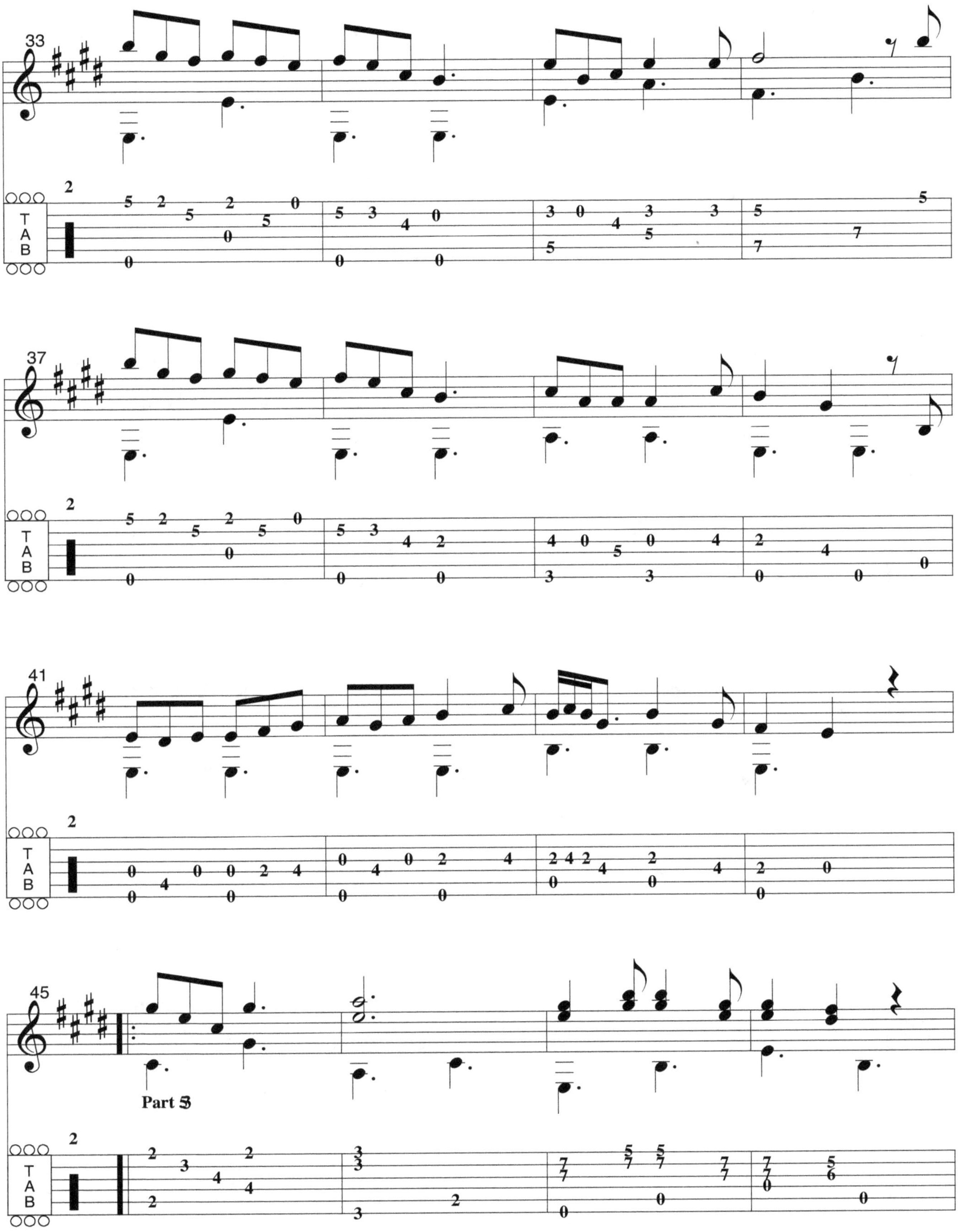
33
TAB
37
TAB
41
TAB
45
TAB

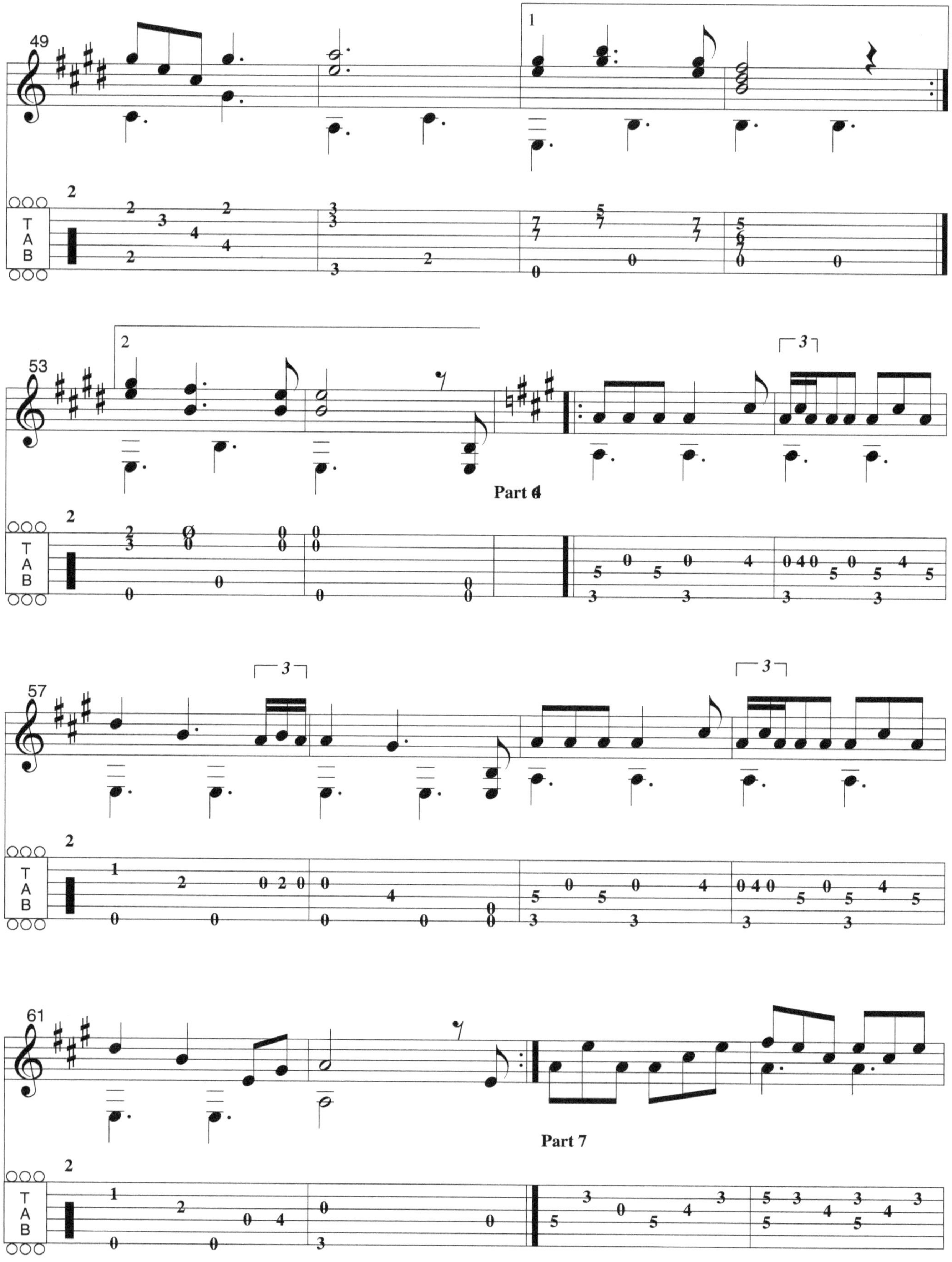
Part 7

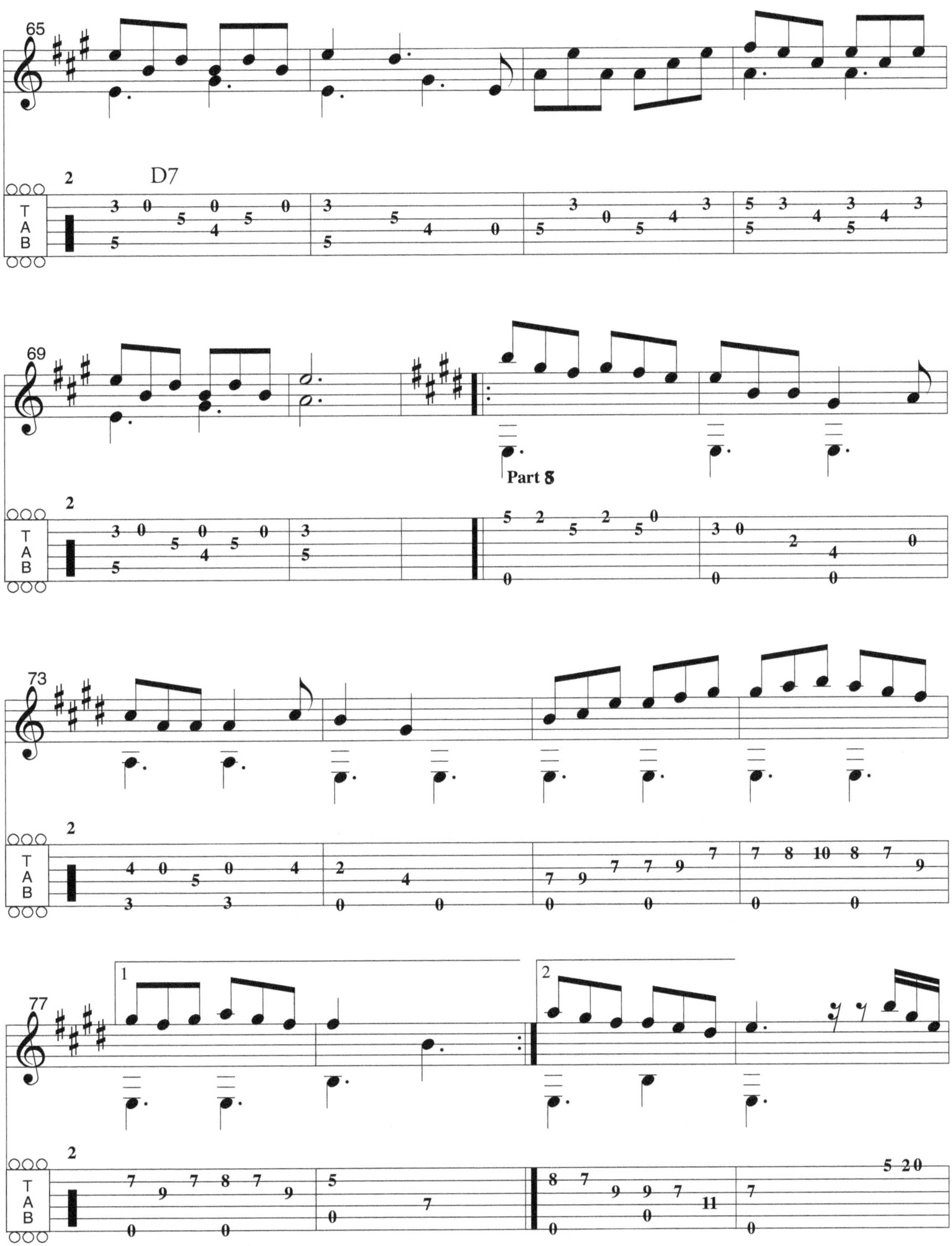
65
D7
TAB
69
Part 8
73
77
1
2

"Music is simple enough. First the instruments are tuned. Then the piece is played to completion in harmony, the notes all clear, and without interruption."

CONFUCIUS

SOME PARTIAL CAPO MATH...

How Many Partial Capo Configurations Are There?

With a universal capo, each string can be capoed or left open at any fret.

To figure how many ways you can put a partial capo on a guitar...

We don't count "0 0 0 0 0 0" which is no strings clamped, and we don't count clamping all 6 strings which is a full capo.

If we solve for

X= the number of configurations
C= the number of capos
F= the number of frets on the instrument
S= the number of strings on the instrument

With one capo it is pretty easy...

Just 2 to the *S* power minus 1, since each of the S strings can be either up or down. So 2 to the 6th power, minus one = 64-1= 63 with at least one string capoed but not all 6.

This means a 6-string guitar yields 63 configurations of one partial capo at each fret. So on a 12 fret neck one universal partial capo can clamp 63 x 12 = **756** configurations, and **882** for a 14-fret neck. It's not easy to get a capo on many guitars at the 14th fret, so it's safe to say **there are 756 ways to put one capo on a guitar, in each tuning.**

It is a lot harder when you use multiple capos, since if more than one capo clamps the same string, only one of them does anything.

"f over c" is "f things taken c at a time" if you remember the formula from math class long ago

$$\text{Then } \mathbf{x} = \binom{f}{c}\left[(c + 1)^{s}-1\right]$$

So with 2 capos we get 66 x 728= **48,048** configurations

and with 3 capos we get = **900,900** configurations

For 12 capos we get = **4,826,808** configurations.

You can also get this same number more easily by thinking like this: The 1st string has 13 different fretting choices on a 12 fret neck (since we count the open string)-- so a 2-string instrument would have (13x13)-1 combinations, and thus a 6-string guitar would have (13x13x13x13x13x13)-1= 4,826,808 configurations. So a 14-fret guitar would yield (15x15x15x15x15x15)-1= 11,390,624 configurations.

This means there are theoretically over 11 million ways to put partial capos on a guitar fingerboard— in every different tuning! Because strings break if you tune them sharp, and they lose tone if you loosen them more than 3-4 frets, the permutations of partial capos is mathematically larger than that of just tunings. There are roughly 5x5x5x5x5x5 tunings (15000+) that you could try with a standard set of strings. I generally find a few dozen useful ways to use capos in each tuning, which leads me to estimate that there are roughly 2000 musically useful capo configurations for every 100 tunings. Since there are about 100 tunings in use, my current research represents about 10-20% of the total size of the "hidden world" of partial capos on a 6-string guitar.

More Musical Resources By Harvey Reid

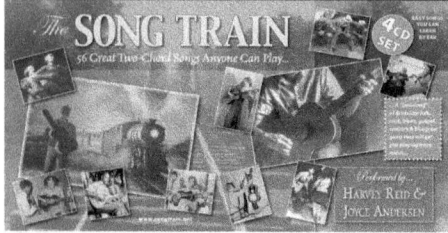

THE SONG TRAIN (2007) is a landmark resource for beginning guitarists by Harvey Reid & Joyce Andersen. 4-CD boxed set with 80-page color hardback book, contains 56 one & two chord songs. Half the songs are copyrighted, by the likes of Bob Dylan, Hank Williams, Chuck Berry etc, so it offers beginners easy but great songs they can play. Folk, blues, gospel, rock, celtic, country and gospel songs, and an amazing cross-section of American music. **www.songtrain.net**

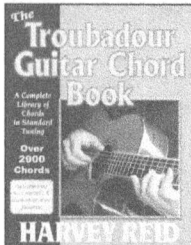

THE TROUBADOUR GUITAR CHORD BOOK (2013) The best, most complete and readable standard-tuning chord encyclopedia, and an essential new reference tool. A monumental and important new work that may never go back on your shelf. Unlike other large chord books that are tailored for jazz guitarists, the *Troubadour Guitar Chord Book* features over 2900 open and closed-string voicings, optimized and selected for solo acoustic and troubadour-style guitarists.

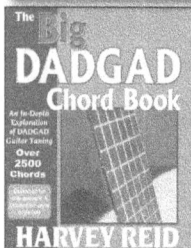

THE BIG DADGAD CHORD BOOK (2014) The best, most complete and readable chord encyclopedia in DADGAD tuning, with 2500 chords mapped out. Another indispensable reference book for anyone who plays in this popular tuning. Also features full-fingerboard diagrams, with every note and scale degree shown for every chord.

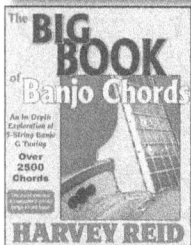

THE BIG BOOK OF BANJO CHORDS (2015) The most complete, detailed and versatile book of chords for standard banjo G tuning. The fingerboard shown like never before, with 5th string notes shown.

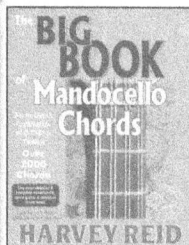

THE BIG BOOK OF MANDOCELLO CHORDS (2015) The most complete, detailed and versatile book of chords for standard C-G-A-D tuning. Also includes 11 of the first ideas ever published for partial capos on mandocello.

THE BIG BOOK OF BARITONE UKULELE CHORDS (2015) The most complete, detailed and versatile book of chords for standard D-G-B-E tuning.

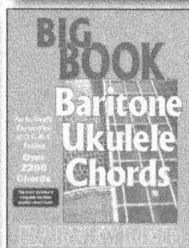

BARITONE UKULELE SIMPLIFIED (2015) Explores 9 different new tunings and partial capo ideas that reveal for the first time how to play instant music with great-sounding but simpler chord shapes. This is the first book to introduce partial capos on a ukulele.

SLEIGHT OF HAND (1983) The first book of partial capo guitar arrangements, still in print. 16 solo guitar arrangements using a universal partial capo. Intermediate to advanced level, mostly for fingerstyle guitar, but has 2 flatpicked fiddle tune arrangements (*Sally Goodin'* and *Devil's Dream*) In TAB and standard notation. *Suite: For the Duchess, Für Elise, Scarborough Fair, Minuet in Dm, Flowers of Edinburgh, Simple Gifts, Sally Goodin', Irish Washerwoman, Pavanne, Minuet in Dm, Red-Haired Boy, June Apple, Jesu Joy of Man's Desiring, Devil's Dream, Sally Goodin', Scherzo, Shenandoah, Greensleeves, Sailor's Hornpipe, Fisher's Hornpipe*

CAPO INVENTIONS (2006) 14 intermediate to advanced arrangements from Reid's catalog of guitar recordings. Precisely transcribed for solo guitar, these pieces all use a 3-string *Esus* type partial capo. In TAB and standard notation. *Skye Boat Song, Highwire Hornpipe, Windy Grave, Hard Times, The Unknown Soldier, Suite: For the Duchess, The Arkansas Traveler, The Minstrel Boy, Red in the Sky, Prelude to the Minstrel's Dream, Norway Suite: Parts 1 &2, Star Island Jig, Macallan's Jig.*

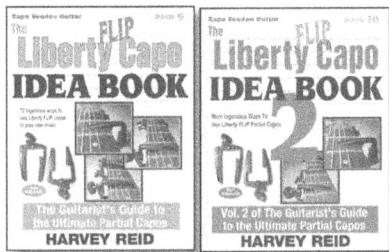

THE LIBERTY "FLIP" CAPO IDEA BOOKS (2014-15) Two volumes, totaling almost 400 pages, with over 113 ideas of partial capo configurations that can be done with a pair of *Model 43* and *Model 65 Liberty* partial capos. These were developed by Harvey Reid, and are the new generation of sleek and versatile partial capos that clamp 6, 5, 4 or 3 strings on most guitars, banjos, ukes and mandolins. Volume I shows 72 ideas, mostly in standard tuning, and with a taste of combining capos with altered tunings. Volume 2 combines capos with altered tunings.

SECRETS OF THE 3-STRING PARTIAL CAPO (2010) 24 mind-bending ways to use the popular 3-string *Esus* (*E-suspended*) type partial capo. *This book may no longer be available after the arrival of the Liberty Capos.* 18 of these ideas are now in the *Liberty Capo IDEA BOOK*, and the other 6 appear in the *Liberty "FLIP" Capo IDEA BOOK Vol.2.*

MORE SECRETS OF THE 3-STRING PARTIAL CAPO (2013) 27 more ways to use 3-string *Esus* (*E-suspended*) type partial capos. **12 of these ideas are now in the *Liberty Capo IDEA BOOK*, and the others are in the *Liberty Capo IDEA BOOK Vol.2.***

SECRETS OF THE 4 & 5-STRING PARTIAL CAPOS (2011) Another treasure trove of ideas, for the *Planet Waves*, *Shubb*, or *Kyser* shortened 4 or 5-string capos. (Also valuable for *Third Hand, Liberty "Flip"* or *Spider* universal capos.) Most people who have one of these capos know a few ways to use them. Here are an amazing 47 ideas that use a 4 or 5-string capo to generate new music. Over 1600 chords. *This book may no longer be available after the arrival of the Liberty Capos.* **30 of these 47 ideas are now in the *Liberty Capo IDEA BOOK*, and the other 17 appear in the *Liberty Capo IDEA BOOK Vol.2.***

SECRETS OF THE 1 & 2-STRING PARTIAL CAPOS (2012) How to use the unique *Woodie's G-Band* 1 and 2-string partial capos. 33 clever ways to use these capos in a number of tunings and in combination with other partial capos, with over 1100 chords. 98 pages are packed with photos, ideas and capo knowledge that is only available here. Even the makers of the capos don't know about these ideas.

SECRETS OF PARTIAL CAPOS IN DADGAD TUNING (2012) Most people think of partial capos as a substitute for open tunings, and don't realize that they can be combined. Harvey Reid shows you over 25 ingenious ways to use partial capos to expand the musical possibilities of DADGAD tuning (4 of them use the similar CGDGAD tuning.) Get new chords, fingerings, voicings, resonances and unlock a new, mysterious world of new music hiding in your fingerboard. **17 of these ideas are now in the *Liberty Capo IDEA BOOK Vol.2.***

SECRETS OF UNIVERSAL PARTIAL CAPOS (2012) 45 ways to get new music from your guitar that can only be done with universal partial capos. This hidden world of music in your fingerboard includes a number of tunings and combinations with other partial capos. Over 1500 chords. Packed with photos, clear explanations and capo strategy will save you years of searching. **Because the *Model 43 Liberty* capo clamps 4 middle strings, 13 of these ideas are now duplicated in the *Liberty Capo IDEA BOOKS, Vol. 1-2.***

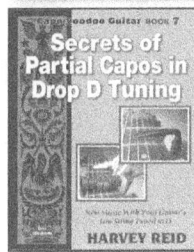

SECRETS OF PARTIAL CAPOS IN DROP D TUNING (2014) The most common tuning is *Drop D*: D A D G B E, and like any tuning, it can be combined with partial capos to add another dimension to the guitar. This book presents 24 ways to use one or more partial capos of all types to generate more new music. **9 of these ideas are now in the *Liberty Capo IDEA BOOK*, and 7 more appear in *Vol.2.*** The others use a universal or *G-Band* capo.

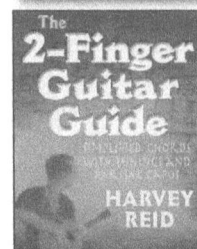

THE LIBERTY GUITAR BEGINNER'S BOOK (2015) Play 30 classic folk songs instantly with super-simple, great-sounding chords. For children or adults, this book carefully explains how to use *Liberty Tuning* to play chords and sing songs in 6 different major and minor keys. You need a guitar, a full capo, and a *Liberty FLIP Model 43* capo.

THE LIBERTY TUNING CHORD BOOK (2013) In his partial capo research, Harvey Reid discovered a simple new guitar tuning that introduces a remarkable geometrical symmetry and simplicity to the guitar fingerboard that no one ever dreamed existed. Here is a thorough examination of what this amazing tuning can do, with over 1200 chords, sorted, mapped out and organized to help you find your way in *Liberty Tuning*. Lots of tips, advice & clear explanations. For guitar teachers, beginners and anyone who already plays guitar and wants to learn about this important discovery.

THE LIBERTY GUITAR METHOD (2013) Total beginners can play music like never before. It's easy to do and sounds great. Learn to use *Liberty Tuning* to play great-sounding, simple 2-finger chords to songs by Bob Dylan, Hank Williams, John Prine, Johnny Cash, Chuck Berry, The Beatles, Adele, and more. You won't believe it 'til you try it. *Hush Little Baby, This Land is Your Land, Your Cheating Heart, A Hard Rain's A Gonna Fall, Amazing Grace, The Cuckoo, Folsom Prison Blues, Angel From Montgomery, Maybellene, Let It Be, Imagine, Someone Like You, The Wedding Song, House of the Rising Sun*

THE LIBERTY SONG TRAIN (2013) Learn how to use *Liberty Tuning* to play all 56 two-chord songs in the epic *Song Train* collection with just 2-finger chords, in the same keys as they were done on the *Song Train* recordings. Beginning guitar has never been easier. Careful explanations, with lots of helpful tips, strategy and advice. If you have the *Song Train* 4-CD collection, you need this companion book.

LIBERTY GUITAR FOR KIDS (2013) It's a huge breakthrough in children's guitar. Children as young as 4 can learn to strum simple 2-finger *Liberty Tuning* chords and play guitar like never before. Classic traditional plus modern children's songs arranged in keys young voices can sing in. No need to wait until the children grow bigger or waste your money on crummy small children's guitars. Learn how even small children can instantly start strumming songs on adult guitars. It's really amazing. *London Bridge, Row Row Row Your Boat, Farmer in the Dell, Hush Little Baby, This Land is Your Land, Oh Susannah, Standing in the Need of Prayer, Hey Lolly Lolly, Comin' Round the Mountain* and more.

THE 2-FINGER GUITAR GUIDE (2013) A careful study of simplified guitar chords, this book takes you through each of the common tunings and partial capo configurations that can be used to play simplified guitar chords. Learn the advantages and disadvantages of each of 28 different guitar environments, including the amazing *Liberty Tuning* and related hybrid tunings. If you have a shortage of fingers on the fretting hand, or if you work with hand injuries, special music education or music therapy, this is the definitive guide to showing what can be done musically with just 2 finger chords.